DIGITAL DESIGN
LAB MANUAL

Jerry D. Daniels
Division of Engineering
Brown University

John Wiley & Sons, Inc.
New York • Chichester • Brisbane • Toronto • Singapore

ISBN 0-471-14686-2

Printed in the United States of America

10 9 8 7 6 5 4 3 2 1

Printed and bound by Bradford & Bigelow, Inc.

CONTENTS

Digital Design LAB MANUAL

PREFACE

This Lab Manual accompanies my textbook *Digital Design from Zero to One.* It presents a personal view of a kit−based lab experience that challenges each student to think about open−ended *design.* The approach is contrasted to step−by−step procedures for building lab circuits.

My Lab Manual places great emphasis on a sequence of carefully written specifications which guide a student from basics of combinational design to more challenging finite state machine designs. The labs were developed over the last twenty years, as an accompaniment to a required course in Digital Circuit Design at Brown University. The present edition has been edited to delete most specific references to the Brown course (EN163 or S163) but otherwise preserves the flavor of the manual as seen by students.

The reader will notice that the CONTRACT GRADING and README.1st file after this Preface still have some time−and−place specific advice for students taking an all−lab course based on this Manual.

The Lab Manual has considerable material on topics such as chip characteristics, A−D conversion, and asynchronous design; topics not covered in *Digital Design from Zero to One*. I have written five supplemental chapters which deal with these subjects; the supplemental chapters are available by ftp from Brown University, or I can print them out and mail them to anyone interested in "adopting" the Lab Manual.

For some years much of the grading of EN163 depended on a student's performance in the lab. See Contract Grading file, next. Briefly, to pass a lab a student had to design, build and demonstrate a circuit which met *all* specifications of the lab (no lab partners were involved) after the demonstration the student had to answer correctly a "fault tolerance question:" What will go wrong with your circuit if I pull out such−and−such a wire? Partial credit for a lab was not possible: grading was binary: either a student got a 1 on the lab by meeting all specs, or the student kept working. Because of this grading structure, the lab writeups themselves had carefully worded specifications, and few hints about how to go about designing the lab. Yes, there would be some general background information (about how a light−emitting diode works, for example, and how to avoid burning it out) but the Lab Manual has little of a "cookbook" feel to it. Each lab has a reference to a chapter in my book *Digital Design from Zero to One*, or to one of the supplemental chapters available by ftp from Brown, and students can leaf through such references if they don't see how to get started with a lab design.

One result of such an emphasis on lab performance: Students confront **design** much more than they would with end−of−chapter problem sets. Because the cost of digital integrated circuit chips is so low, and because it's the nature of digital chips to be forgiving about circuit noise and power supply tolerance, students in a digital design lab get a unique opportunity to build in hardware answers to problems that in other engineering courses would have to be worked out on paper. Individual engineering departments and the national Accrediting Board for Engineering and Technology (ABET) both put weight on *design* as an important factor in engineering education. A well structured digital design lab can be in the educational spotlight when it comes to design content.

Software. As straightforward as it is to layout and build digital circuits, using white plastic breadboard, DIP chips and solid−core hookup wire, it is even easier to bring up various layout and simulation programs, then point and click your way to a successful design. In the labs as I teach it at Brown, I have come to favor software which has less overhead for learning−−wiring methods that are intuitive; labelling conventions that are not restrictive; file structure that does not have to be worried about, etc. As a result, I use MacBreadboard 1.16, LogicWorks 2.5 and Beige Bag 3.0 software in the course. All of the software is networked on Apple Macintosh or Power PC computers. Some of the labs (for example, the hex multiplier) can be done either in hardware or software. Other labs, such as successive approximation A−D, must be done in hardware because the simulators have no analog components. At any rate, we have tried in the past to work with more "industrial strength" layout and simulation software, such as PowerView from ViewLogic Inc., and/or XACT from Xilinx, but found the learning time and frustration factor too great for a one semester introduction to digital logic. If we had more access to Sun workstations we might try DigLog from Caltech. The closest we come to standard engineering software is PALASM for use in programming PALs such as 22V10s. PALASM is used on PC clones hooked up to a programming station. We have a separate progaramming station for EPROMs, also PC−based.

MATLAB software is used in chapter 1 of *Digital Design from Zero to One*, and is mentioned in chapter 3 with regard to computer methods for minimizing truth tables. At this time there are no particular labs that students do in number conversion, other than various end−of−chapter exercises for text chapters 1 and 3.

Logic Analyzer. Students in a digital design course should become familiar with a logic analyzer as an important troubleshooting instrument. In the lab at Brown we have HP1651As available. From the beginning, each student is given a *logic probe* and soon becomes at ease using the hand−held logic probe to troubleshoot simple circuits. Later, especially for the succssive approximation lab, and the FSM multiplier, it becomes tedious to single−step a clock and look one by one at various latch and flip flop outputs. Students come to see a logic analyzer as a logic probe on steroids. The drawback to the 1651A is the "overhead learning" a student needs to do to get something useful out of the machine. Most students accept that the effort is worth the reward in learning a more efficient way to look at multi−output FSMs.

In addition to logic analyzers on carts, in the lab at Brown are 386 or 486 machines for PROM programming and for programming PALs with PALASM. There are also soldering irons, and spools of 22 gauge solid core hookup wire, and bins with extra hardware and chips, for "self−service" replacement of parts.

Getting started. At a certain level, the information in this lab manual may provide the reader with inspiration to go out and try some of the experiments him or herself. At a more practical level, the labs here assume the student has a kit of the chips and hardware listed in the inventory, and has access to data sheets about the chips. Some, but not all, of the material may be already available at a University stockroom, or at a local Radio Shack. I list other sources below.

Where to get parts. Radio Shack is one place, but it's relatively expensive. For me, some things, such as wire strippers, come from local electronic/hardware stores. Digikey, in Minnesota, is a good place for many items, from chips to switches to potentiometers. Various distributors, such as Arrow, Wiley and Hamilton−Avnet, are good for hard−to−get memory chips and Analog Devices chips. The keyboards come directly from Texas Instruments. 22V10 PALs were kindly donated by AMD. Breadboard and power supplies are from Global Specialties or their distributors. Wavetek multimeters we purchase from Contact East. The direct plug−in hex displays are from Hewlett Packard. The LF353 op amp is a National Semiconductor part.

This edition of the lab manual does not have all the data sheets a student would need to learn about chip pinouts. The data sheets I copy for students at Brown are from catalogs of **Signetics, Analog Devices, National Semiconductor, Texas Instruments (TI), Motorola, Intel, Siliconix, Advanced Micro Devices (AMD)** and **Hitachi.**

Since some of the labs (like Lab 5, chip characteristics) depend on reading the Supplemental Chapters not in the text. You can either get the chapters from the ftp site at Brown Engineering, or I can copy them off and mail them to you. E−mail me at internet node below. A couple of the labs, particularly the CPU lab and the FPGA lab, have not been used by me for a few years; they are included in the manual for the sake of completeness, and for those who might want to work the labs into a more modern form.

Some of the material in the first part of the lab manual helps beginners get started stripping wire, orienting chips, testing power supplies etc. Another good reference on tips for designing digital hardware is:

Robert Seidensticker, *The Well−Tempered Digital Design*, Addison−Wesley, Reading, MA (1988).

An excellent video about the manufacture of integrated circuits was produced by Texas Instruments in the early 1990s. *From Sand to Circuit* is shown in my class about half way through the semester, as a break from round−the−clock digital circuit building. TI in 1996 came out with a new video, *Making of a Microchip*. Call 214−917−2505. Cost is $179.

I hope you enjoy (or at least find educational) my lab manual. A lab component is important to any course in digital design. The labs here range from straightforward to frustrating and rewarding, and their order of appearance in the manual is along that axis.
My e−mail address is

```
jdd@en355.engin.brown.edu
```

and I would appreciate any comments about the lab manual.

This edition of the lab manual refers to labs by number. For example, Lab 9 always refers to the successive approximation lab.

Selection of labs. In this manual I print out most of the labs I've used over the past two decades. There are more labs than can be finished in one semester than all but the brightest student working full time could do. I see two kinds of choices to offer: One, a set of Labs for a lab component of a text−based course; two, a set of labs for a total lab course in digital design, a concept which i have used at times with good reaction from students.

Suggested SET OF LABS TO ACCOMPANY A LECTURE COURSE:

Lab 0	One Bit Full Adder
Lab 1	Multiplexed Display
Lab 4K	Keyboard Encoding
Lab 5	Chip Input−Output
Lab 6C	Content−addressable Memory
Lab B	4 bit X 4 bit Hex Multiplier
Lab 12	Tape Controller

SET OF LABS FOR FULL SEMESTER OF LAB WORK:

Lab 0.1	Two Bit Subtractor
Lab 1	Multiplexed Display
Lab 2	4−bit 2C Squarer
Lab 3M or Lab 3P: more combinational design	
Lab 4S	Sequencer with External Control
Lab 4K	Keyboard Encoding
Lab 5	Chip Input−Output Measurements
Lab 6C or 6D: Memory	
Lab 8	Multiplying DAC
Lab 9	Successive Approximation A−D Converter
Lab A	Serial Transmission and Error Correction
Lab B	4 bit X 4 bit Hex Multiplier
Lab C0, C*	Asynchronous router and Microprogrammer
Lab D	Traffic Light Controller
Lab E	PAL for Elevator Control
Lab 11	Asynchronous Shepard
Lab 12	Tape Controller
Lab 13	Soo Locks Controller

A steady state condition. For the labs to be as free of *needless* frustration as possible, it is important for me to have a few Teaching Assistants who took the course the previous year. Also, a good inventory of spare parts keeps students from panicking when too many chips burn out.

Grading Contract

Grading standards

I tell you now, at the beginning of the course, what is required for C, B, A and A+ grades. Grading is by contract, not on the curve. How rapidly or slowly other students advance in the course will not affect your grade.

Your grade will be determined by your ability to design and build solutions to lab challenges (and secondarily by problem sets, and by oral quizes). You will keep a scorecard on which we will sign off completed labs.

• First, to be issued your kit, do lab 0.1, "2–Bit Subtractor," on MacBreadboard. MacBreadboard is a layout and simulation program available on Macintoshes in rooms 340 and 450, and off the server in the CIT. For more information, see next part of Lab Manual, **READ-ME.first**, under the section "Getting Started."

• To pass the course with a grade of **S** or **C**, do labs 0.1, 1, 3P, 4K, 4S, 6C, B and 12, *and* receive Satisfactory scores on 4 out of 6 homework assignments.

• To qualify for a **B**, meet the requirements for a C **and do labs 5, 9, and *one* of labs A, D, E, 13,** *and* receive Satisfactory scores on 4 out of 6 homework assignments.

• To qualify for an **A**, meet the requirements for a B **and do labs 2, 8, C0 and C* and 4 out of 6 homework assignments.**

• For the honor of an **A+ = A⟋** complete the requirements for an A *and* do any one more lab by 5 pm of the last Monday of the term.

  • Brown regulations limit the number of A's with distinction to 20% of enrollment.
  • You will receive a *Certificate suitable for framing*.
  • At the time you finish your A+ you will be deputized as an **Honorary Teaching Assistant** who can sign off other students' labs for the last week of class.
  • Think about being a S163 TA for next year!
  • Think about **Independent Study** with JD, working on evolutionary algorithms for minimization of truth tables (see end of chapter 3 in the text).

S163 Exclusion Principle

For each day the course is in session you may have only one lab signed off. You can, however, complete more than one lab per day. The other labs will be signed off in *the future,* starting with the next weekend. For the last week of class, there is no "future."

Lab not open, Professor not available, on weekends.

Be aware that the scheduling structure of this course can confuse students: In a traditional course you sometimes can work haphazardly during the term, then study hard for the final, and still pull a good grade. Such a strategy would be futile in S163.

Only one of each chip per design

In building any lab, you can use **only** the chips in your kit. In other words, you can use *only one* of each chip on the inventory list. Don't "borrow" extra chips from a friend or from the drawers just because you need a few more NAND gates to complete your design. Your design won't count if you use more than one of any chip. See "Circuit Construction Guidelines" for tips on how to find more gates and registers in your kit.

Partial Credit

There is no partial credit. This can be a source of frustration.

First, requirements for each lab must be met completely. For example, Lab Nine (successive approximation converter) calls for a sequential display of 0, 1, 2, 3, 4, 5, 6, 7 etc, as you turn a potentiometer knob. If you are able to display only 0, 1, 2, 3, 4, 5, 7..., then Lab Nine cannot be signed off until you troubleshoot your circuit and get that **6** on the display, in proper sequence between 5 and 7. We do not require continuous perfection, however. If your circuit, for example, shows 0, 1, 2, 3, 4, 5, 6, 7 as little as 50% of the time, that's okay.

Second, the requirements of the grades are fixed. For example, one lab short of the **A** requirements nets you a **B**.

Incompletes

An incomplete grade can be granted if the student makes arrangements with the Dean of Summer Studies. Generally, serious medical problems are grounds for an incomplete. Since I am not around after the end of the summer session, an incomplete is best made up the following summer, when S163 is open for business again.

The Fault Tolerance Question (FTQ)

The requirements for each lab are spelled out later in the Lab Manual. When you demonstrate a circuit, we will verify that it meets all requirements. Then we will ask you a question about your circuit—The Fault Tolerance Question. If you answer the FTQ correctly, then we will sign your scorecard and shake your hand.

Think carefully about your FTQ—if you do not answer it correctly then we will be obliged to ask you <u>two</u> more FTQ's, both of which you must answer correctly in order to have your scorecard signed. For every FTQ missed, two more must be asked. This, however, will not go on for long. If you miss three FTQ's we will match the *id* numbers on the solderless breadboards of your circuit with the numbers of the breadboards checked out to you. If the numbers do not match, we will ask you if you know how to spell *plagiarism*. If you are guilty of attempting to demonstrate a circuit someone else designed and built, *with little knowledge yourself of the circuit's workings,* then your case will be brought to the attention of the Dean of Summer Studies for disciplinary action. Of course, if you think you have a thorough knowledge of someone else's circuit, you can *risk* demonstrating it for credit!

Suppose you have missed three FTQ's with your own circuit. Just go home, study your circuit for a day, and try again. Perhaps you didn't document the circuit on paper, and became confused during the FTQ episode. You don't need to hand us your documentation, but it can prove useful during the FTQ! [Certainly proper documentation is important in a research or industrial setting, but in this course our philosophy allows you to do the minimum set of circuit drawings necessary to help you answer the FTQ, then go on to worry about the next lab challenge design.]

The FTQ can take one of three forms:
1. We may ask you **what (and only what) will happen if a particular wire is removed** from your circuit. Or we may reverse two wires and ask what will go wrong. Think about your answer, explain it carefully, <u>then</u> let <u>us</u> pull out the wire to see if you are right. We will not choose power or ground lines to individual chips, but otherwise any connection is fair game. Note that if you claim some particular result Z will be wrong after the FTQ wire is pulled and Z does *not* malfunction then you *miss* the question. You should have an understanding of how an input might "float" if it's unconnected. You are allowed to inspect the current state of your circuit with a logic probe or voltmeter, but you are not allowed to change inputs, or send in clock signals, until the answer is tested.

You may want to give your FTQ answer in the form of contingencies: "If X is the input, then Y is the output; if W is the input, the Z is the output." Vague answers like, "The circuit won't work," or "The same thing happened to a friend of mine," are not satisfactory. Also unsatisfactory are answers like, "I've got to go eat lunch now." Please allow at least 15 minutes for an FTQ. Once the FTQ process starts it cannot be interrupted, or your lack of answer is counted as a miss. **We will pull out the wire, after we understand your answer. Don't experiment with the wire yourself**...if we find you've pulled the wire out before we do, we must ask you a different FTQ, such as...

2. We may ask you to **turn your back while we pull out or rearrange wires**. You then have 15 minutes to get your circuit working again, in our presence. Note that with this FTQ you do not have to verbalize an answer, you can simply turn your right brain loose to fix the problem. If you cannot get your mutilated circuit working while we're present, then take it home, repair it at your leisure, and appear the next day for a different FTQ. Of course before you take it home we'll want to check your breadboard id numbers to make sure someone else didn't build "your" circuit.
3. Or we may ask you a question from one of the end–of–chapter exercises in *Digital Design from Zero to One*—Don't complain! If this were a regular engineering course such questions

would be on your problem sets and exams all the time! At any rate, if we choose a type–3 question, it will be relevant to the lab you're demonstrating.

The above approaches—pulled wire, mutilated circuit and text question—are the three **primary** FTQ techniques. Other forms of questions may be appropriate for particular labs. For example, we may ask you to demonstrate a digital multimeter (DMM) measurement for lab 5, or we may ask you what voltage will result if we alter a resistor in lab 8, or you may be asked to compute a Hamming code correction for lab B. For lab 4, done on Logic–Works software, you may be asked about replacing one gate with another kind. At any rate we may use our discretion to choose the FTQ; Miss Manners would scold you for protesting the unfairness of any particular question.

During your FTQ do not let the hurly burly atmosphere of the lab make you anxious. We may be wandering from one student to another to make efficient use of our time. For you, getting the first question right can save a lot of anguish! Remember—with none of the traditional written tests in this course, the FTQ is the only way we have of verifying your knowledge of digital circuit design. Over the duration of the course you may spend 2–6 hours answering FTQ's.

Collaboration

There are no lab partners in this course; you have sufficient parts, including multimeter, logic probe and power supply, to do all the labs on your own. While you must figure out the answer your FTQ alone, prior to a demonstration and FTQ you are welcome to collaborate with your fellow students. Doing so, in fact, may be part of your learning experience in the course. Beware that worthwhile collaboration ends at the point where you simply copy the wiring on someone else's board without understanding its particular design. *In that case you run a great risk of failing your FTQ.*

Public display of grades

We will keep a whiteboard near the entrance to the lab; each student will be a row and each lab and homework assignment will be a column on the board. After finishing a lab your row will receive a ✓ in the lab's column. The white board will be a public record of each student's progress.

Finishing the course

Turn in your scorecard and your kit, including all extra breadboard checked out If you wish to keep parts from your kit, pay for them according to the prices on the inventory sheet. Otherwise, replace the chips back into the drawers from whence they came.
Place toggle switches, potentiometers and DIP switches back in the colored bins.
Your grade will be listed as incomplete until you account for your kit.
We'll be especially interested to see your voltmeter, logic probe and power supply.
We also want to check in the display chip 7433, the EPROM, the 22V10 PAL, the 7576 ADC and the 7340 HEX display and wire strippers.

Scorecard

NAME_____

meter_____
logic probe_____
power supply_____
stripper_____

Board #1_____ #2_____ #3_____ #4_____ #5_____ #6_____

Lab		DATE	CHECKER
−1	Destroy a display		
0.1	2−bit subtractor with borrow−in		*
1	Common−cathode multiplexed display		
2SQ	4−bit 2C squarer		
3P	Priority Alarm (or 3M Majority Logic)		
4K	16 button matrix keyboard encoding		
4S	Sequencer with External Control		
5	Analysis of input & output for logic families		*
6C	Content−addressable memory		
7	Time Stamper		
8	Exponential Decay with Multiplying DAC		
9	4−bit A→D converter using successive approx.		*
A	Serial Transmission & Error Correction		
B	4−bit x 4−bit Positive Number Multiplier		
C0	Subroutine return timing		
C*	Emulation of 2911 Sequencer		*
D	Traffic Light Square Dance		
E	Elevator Controller		
F_{16}	Electronic Synapse		
10_{16}	Digital filter, high pass		
11_{16}	Asynchronous shepherd		
12_{16}	Tape Count Controller		
13_{16}	Soo Locks Controller		

GRADE [ ]

* = must be signed by JD

This file contains some general-purpose and some Brown University-specific advice for students taking an all-lab course in digital design.

README.1st

When people speak in awe about the rapid pace of technological change, a favorite example is digital electronics. Beginning in 1948 with the transistor and currently manifested in large−scale integrated circuits, a series of improvements in semiconductor technology has taken modern society from the industrial age to the computer age. These improvements have resulted in orders of magnitude price reductions of logic gates so that more and more hardware has become less and less costly. In this course we will take advantage of the low cost of integrated circuits (IC's). Instead of working out problems with pencil and paper, you will be issued a bag of IC chips and other useful components, and with your Bag−O−Chips kit (and computer layout and simulation software) you will design and build answers to a series of lab challenges.

Missing from this course are many activities usually found in Engineering courses. You take no mid−term exam and no final exam. No calculus is involved. There are no lab reports to generate. Formal lectures are replaced by the text, and by interaction in the lab. Emphasis is on your hardware and software solutions to the lab challenges. After you demonstrate a successful circuit and answer correctly a question about its performance, A TA or I will sign your scorecard. No documentation is required (although it may come in handy answering your circuit performance question). You can build your designs whenever and wherever you like. By completing successively more labs, you qualify automatically for C, B, A, and A with distinction.

Good news and bad news

With such a teaching method, there are good news and bad news. The **good news** is that you spend all of your time thinking about design and getting hands−on experience realizing your ideas in hardware. After each successful lab, you may feel an elevation of mood—a potent and immediate sense of accomplishment, more so than you would handing in a problem set or finishing a clocked exam.

The **bad news** is that you must learn to budget your time to make steady progress. There are no real deadlines other than the end of the course! Few hints are provided in the lab manual, but you can pick up a great deal useful information by reading the text. You must learn to deal with the frustrations of designing and debugging circuits which are reluctant to perform for you. Sometimes it will seem that you have exhausted all feasible approaches to a problem, and there will be no error messages for you to study.

There is a lot to learn. At first it may seem like you're drinking from a fire hose, but by the time the course is over you will have learned a great deal—either you will have taken advantage of the good news and learned a lot about digital and interface circuit design, or the bad news will have taken its toll and you will have learned a lot about procrastination and self-deception. Fortunately, the first choice makes more sense than the second!

The textbook. Feel free to offer suggestions for improvement of *Digital Design from Zero to One*. Remember—I've written the book for the benefit of students like you, so if *anything* is unclear, let me know! Please ask me whatever questions you like about the reading; point out any deficiencies in explanation you may find. Your advice will help with the second edition!

Computer help: There will be a couple computer sessions in the second week where you will be introduced to Macintosh layout and simulation software: MacBreadboard, LogicWorks, Beige Bag. Otherwise, the TA is available in the lab, in the afternoon.

e-mail. I read the bulletin board `engin.discuss` every day, if you'd like to post something there about this course. Or you can send me e-mail directly to
`jdd@en355.engin.brown.edu`
I will to create a batch file of student e-mail addresses from which I can send out general announcements about this course.

Lab supplies & tools

If a chip in your kit is defective, we'll replace it without question. About 5% of the "experienced" chips in our inventory may have problems. Consider the possibility of a defective chip as you troubleshoot malfunctioning circuits.

Resistors and capacitors can be had from bins and spools. Various colors of 22−24 gauge solid core hook−up wire will also be available in the lab.

The lab will contain several large power supply−logic probe stations to allow you to troubleshoot your designs expeditiously and thoroughly. You may need to use the lab power supplies if your circuit requires more power than the portable power unit in the kit can deliver. Oscilloscopes, function generators, HP 1651A logic analyzers and a PROM programmer are also available for student use.

There will be soldering irons in the labs, for connecting wires to keyboard, toggle switch, and potentiometer leads. Read "Soldering Tips" in the Lab Manual for advice about how to use the soldering iron.

We aim to provide good service in this course. For example, instead of a few cheap multimeters lying around the lab, probably with a dead batteries, burned out fuses, missing probes and no instruction manual, you each will have a $119 multimeter with a fresh battery, working fuse, good probe cables and handy instruction manual. Is there anything else we can do for you?

"Time is Nature's way of preventing everything from happening all at once."

Difficulty of the Labs

Different students will find different labs more or less easy, but here is my view of how much effort is required: Labs 1 – 8 are progressively more challenging, in fact their numbers are about equal to how many hours you might spend getting them done, (four hours for lab 4, etc).

Labs 9 thru F_{16} are all designed to be at about the same level difficulty, I'd guess about a dozen hours apiece. Labs 10_{16}, 11_{16} and 12_{16} are a little different, and may take less time if you appreciated the methods involved.

Another thought: In some ways the labs are like programming assignments in CS classes, where the chips play the role of the CS language instructions; the more familiar you become with the chips, the more effectively you can do the labs.

Getting started

Paul:	*How does this thing start?*
Old Fred:	*It starts with a Blue Meanie attack.*
Paul:	*Well...what if there're no Blue Meanies?*
Old Fred	*Then you...uh...you look for a switch...*

from *YELLOW SUBMARINE*

Your Blue Meanies are the lab challenges. Before you attempt to finish one, you need to get started...maybe find a switch.

Read chapter 1 of the text. Study the requirements for Lab 0.1; think about binary adding and subtracting. On paper, work out a design for Lab 0.1; The Lab 0.1 write–up introduces you to MacBreadboard. Find MacBreadboard software on a Mac. Familiarize yourself with selecting chips and connecting wires. "Build" your design for Lab 0.1 on MacBreadboard and demonstrate it to us. If it doesn't work immediately, use the logic probe feature of MacBreadboard to troubleshoot your circuit. After it works, answer correctly a FTQ and have your scorecard signed. Proceed to assemble your hardware kit!

Your kit

When you are ready for your kit, assemble the parts from the drawers in the lab. Don't take more than one chip from each drawer, and follow the inventory list (**"basic kit"**) in the Lab Manual. For parts like your potentiometer, keyboard, and toggle switch, you may need to use the soldering iron to attach wires to their pins. Don't forget wire and strippers. Ask us for help with the soldering iron, if you need it. We'll check out breadboard, logic probe and power supply to you, and write down which ones you have on your scorecard. For lab 5 you check out a multimeter, and after lab 5 you pick up more chips, listed on the 2nd inventory sheet.

Second Lab. Practice stripping wire and pushing it into the holes of the breadboard. Understand how the holes in the breadboard are connected internally. Try assembling and testing a design for Lab 1.

If your hardware design doesn't seem to perform properly, troubleshoot it. First make sure the power supply is on and that +5v & ground are properly connected to the pins of your chips. Double–check your design, and its wiring. Use a logic probe to measure internal logic levels, making sure signals are propagating correctly and your chips are okay. Read the Circuit Constructions Guideline in the Lab Manual.

In building any lab, you can use only **the chips in your kit. In other words, you can use** _only one_ **of each chip on the inventory list. Don't "borrow" extra chips from a friend or from the drawers just because you need a few more NAND gates to complete your design. Your design won't count if you use more than one of any chip.** See "Circuit Construction Guidelines" for tips on how to find more gates and registers in you kit.

Replacing chips: **Don't throw "bad" chips in the trash! Usually the chip isn't bad, it's you're wiring that's wrong! Give the "defective" chip to me or a TA and we'll save it to test later!**

Digital design from zero to one

During the first week of this course you may feel you have been pushed off the deep end of the pool and are immersed in too much digital electronics—600 pages of text, 400 pages of lab manual, 30 different IC chips and their data sheets, layout & simulation software, etc. Yes, you are in the deep end, but you will become aware that your feet can touch the bottom, and there are no calculus barracudas swimming around. In other words, that's all there is; it's just pushing 1's and 0's around; using logical AND, OR and NOT in various combinations. By the third week of this course you may have a different "problem"—becoming obsessed with the streamlined beauty of digital circuit design and spending all your time arranging chips and colored wire on your breadboards, immersing yourself in the flow* of one lab after another, neglecting your other courses.

Digital Design Lab Manual

Finishing the course

Turn in your scorecard and your kit, including all extra breadboard checked out If you wish to keep parts from your kit, pay for them according to the prices on the inventory sheet. Otherwise, replace the chips back into the drawers from whence they came.

Place toggle switches, potentiometers and DIP switches back in the colored bins.

Your grade will be listed as incomplete until you account for your kit.

We'll be especially interested to see your voltmeter, logic probe and power supply.

We also want to check in the display chip 7433, the EPROM, the 22V10 PAL, the 7576 ADC and the 7340 HEX display and wire strippers.

> That's all folks!

---

* Flow in the psychological sense, as popularized by Seymour Papert in *Mindstorms,* Basic Books, 1982. And see the book, *Flow—The Psychology of Optimal Experience*, Mihaly Csikszentmihalyi, Harper, 1991.

Circuit Construction Guidelines
& Advice for dealing with frustration

We assume you've figured out how to strip wire, and have soldered wires to your toggle switch, potentiometer, and keyboard. You have access to a digital multimeter (DMM) to measure resistance and capacitance (or maybe you've broken the resistor color code!) You've found out how your power supply works, in connection with its target breadboard, and how the logic probe should be connected to +5v and ground for proper operation. You know which holes are connected to which on the white plastic breadboard.

Getting organized

Be a little compulsive. Arrange the parts in your kit so that you don't waste time looking through the entire lot each time you need a particular chip. You should lay down a bit of aluminum foil to press the pins of the CMOS chips and VMOS transistors onto; this will short their pins together and prevent the chip gates from being blown by high–voltage static electricity.

Glance at some of the data sheets for chips in your kit. You'll want to study (memorize?) functions of the various chips, so you'll know what it's possible for the chips to do in solution of the design problems you're confronted with. For purposes of study, you can divide the chips into **combinational** and **sequential** (depending on whether or not the chip has flip flops). Study the combinational chips first. In some ways the chips are like instructions in a computer language...you'd have a difficult time writing a program without knowing the instruction set...
Most important about each chip is the pinout—which pin is assigned which operation; some pins are input, some output, and two are for power and ground. Along with the data sheet's pinout, a truth table or timing diagram may be included to help you understand the inner workings of a particular chip. The DC (static) characteristics of some inverter chips will concern you in lab 5.

It may be helpful to make up 3 X 5 cards with pin–outs of the chips. With these you will not have to keep leafing through your data sheets to connect one chip to another. All of the cards necessary for a circuit can be laid out on a table top and you can double–check quickly that each pin has been connected properly.

If you are in doubt about how a particular chip works, don't hesitate to hook it up in a small test situation, apart from the main design you may be working on.

Starting your design

It is a good idea to begin your work with a design on paper; leave plenty of white space so you can red–pencil in corrections. Before you start building, work through a typical input to see if your design on paper gives the correct response. You might also try our Macintosh-based layout/simulators, such as MacBreadboard, which can allow further tests of a circuit before wiring it up. Of course, with the solderless breadboard hardware, wiring does not take long and changes can be made easily.

Assembling your circuit: Do it neatly, with wires that are not so long that they rise up above the breadboard in one confused mass, but not so short that they loop directly over the tops of chips and prevent you from popping out individual chips to test for defectives. **Do not pull a chip out of the breadboard with your fingers!** The pins are liable to bend. Insert something like a bobbie-pin under the chip and *pry the chip out gently*. You may want to invest in a pair of pliers which can grip firmly your 22 gauge solid core hook-up wire while you strip the insulation from the ends. If you cut your wire at an angle, the ends will have points that will more easily slip into the breadboard holes. See Discussion of Lab Zero for illustration of solderless breadboard connections. Use a consistent color coding scheme for your wires – – all white for +5V; all green for ground, etc.; use a variety of colors to aid troubleshooting. For parallel lines of information (buses) you may wish to use wire colors corresponding to something systematic, like the rainbow. Remember to conserve your wire. We buy "only" about 100 feet per student!

If you are building a complex circuit, try to do it modularly. Build the display first, the input, next, then timing control, etc. That is, break the problem into small sections and do one section at a time—bottom-up circuit building...like structured programming! Test each section before you go on to the next.

Logic probes and logic analyzers

Logic Probes. Each student should have his or her own logic probe, which attaches by two cables to a 5 volt power supply. The logic probe is your first weapon in troubleshooting a digital circuit. With it you can tell quickly the voltage-logic levels in your circuit. The LO LED (red) is on for voltages less than about 0.8 volt; the HI LED (green) lights at a threshold greater than about 2.2 v. If the logic probe tip is unconnected or if it is measuring a voltage between 0.8 and 2.2 volts neither of the LED's will light. <u>The logic probe will blink when it is detecting a pulse train</u>.

EPROM. For some of the later labs, we will supply you with an EPROM (Erasable Programmable Read-Only Memory) chip; you can observe the UV erasing, and the programming process on the IBM PC.

Logic Analyzers. You will have access to a Hewlett Packard 1651A logic analyzer—a device which can keep track of many digital signals simultaneously. The logic analyzer is more awkward to hook up than a simple logic probe, but it is a more power troubleshooting weapon. You can generally track down any timing or logic problem in this course with the HP 1651A. You can introduce yourself to logic analyzers by reading the HP booklet "Feeling Comfortable with Logic Analyzers."

"Stop me before I burn out another chip."—always double-check that you have the proper polarity of power before turning on your circuit. *Reversal of the power supply leads* (that is, putting +5 to ground in your circuit and ground to your +5 rail) *could damage all the chips in your circuit!* Except for your LF 353 op amp and 654 VCO, your chips can all be powered by +5v. Any time you work on your circuit, turn off the power. It's not that your power supply is dangerous to you, but an inadvertent touching of a live power wire to the wrong chip pin might blow out the chip. Another example: putting the wrong polarity input to a 654 VCO can destroy the chip by reverse-biasing the input transistor.

Power Supplies

Each student can have a Global Specialties "Proto Board 10" power supply plus bread board system. This supply is capable of delivering 1 amp of current at 5 volts. It also has ±12 volts at ¼ amp. As you can see on your Proto Board 10, it appears that the +5 volts and ground are awkwardly placed together on nearby rails. This placement is actually for a good reason. **It's possible to blow out the 5 volt supply by connecting it directly to the +12 volt supply. Be careful! Don't do connect two power supply outputs together!** These supplies are not equipped with over-voltage protection. Also, the Proto Board 10 has no on-off switch; we suggest un-plugging the supply while you work on your circuit, then double-checking the power supply wires before plugging it in again. And the Proto Board 10 has no power indicator light; if it appears you power supply isn't functioning, even though it's plugged in, try disconnecting the power supply from the breadboard, and seeing if your logic probe works. If your logic probe doesn't light up when touched to +5 volts, try measuring voltage with the DMM. If you can't read +5v, bring your power supply to us for a decent burial.

Other power supplies. Some students will receive Global Specialties model 203 power supplies plus breadboard. And the lab room has several large power supplies + logic probes which you can hook in to. If your power supply malfunctions or if you simply want to have a second voltage source, there are other things you can do. You could put four nickel cadmium batteries in series, recharging them when the voltage drops. Or you may be able to find an AC adapter that will produce a voltage in the proper range close enough to 5v. Or you may wish to use a battery with a voltage greater than 5v (say a 9v battery or a 9v adapter) and attach the battery to a 5v regulator. A regulator is a 3 pin chip — one pin takes your higher-than-5v input; another pin is ground; and the third pin provides a *regulated* 5v output. You can buy a 5v regulator (7805) for about $1.00 from Radio Shack. The battery solution to the power supply problem is marginal. A more standard electrical engineering approach is shown below:

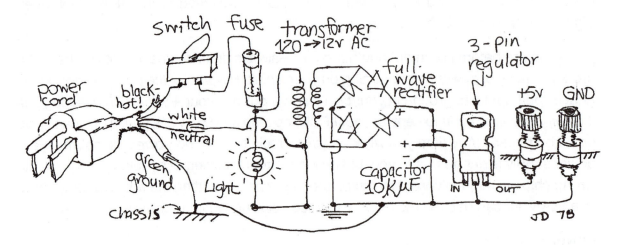

INSIDE OF A POWER SUPPLY

Here you provide a *power cord* which leads into a grounded *chassis box* with a *switch*, a *fuse*, and a *light* on the hot power wire. From there the 120v line power is applied to a *transformer* which steps the alternating voltage down to about 12v rms. The transformer output feeds a *full wave rectifier* which makes the waveform all positive; a large *capacitor* across the output of the diode bridge removes much of the ripple from the signal. Finally the *unregulated dc* voltage is applied to a *5v regulator,* which gives you the proper voltage output. All of this can be housed in a sturdy grounded box with the wires soldered together at terminal strips; convenient *binding posts* can make +5v and ground available for your circuits. Most conservative choice for your ground is the **green wire** from the power cord; this connects unequivocally to power company ground, and won't be confused with the white "neutral" wire; ideally the green connection should be to the shielding chassis only, and not normally carry current, but here you can play it safe another way...be careful.

The parts for such a power supply can be purchased for about $20 from a place like Radio Shack, or as kit PRO–1 (#7001) from Global Specialties, New Haven, CT 06512. A soldering iron and pliers are available in the lab, for assembling your custom power supply.

Breadboard

The holes in EXP–300 breadboard are connected as shown in the accompanying xerox. All the holes in top row "X" are connected together, as are all the holes in the bottom row "Y." Normally you run a wire from +5 volts on the power supply to "X," and another wire from Ground to "Y." Straddle a chip across the trough in the middle of the board, and press its pins into holes in rows "E" and "F." Each set of A–E holes is connected together, as is each set of F–J holes. Thus each pin from the chip is accessible through four other holes,

Digital Design Lab Manual

either A–D or G–J. For example, if you've pressed your 14 pin 7400 chip into columns 1–7, then you can run a wire from a hole in row "X" to hole A1 and you will have provided your chip with +5 v. Likewise a wire from a hole in row "Y" to hole J7 will ground your chip. Note the orientation of pin 1 on the chip in the xerox. There is more information about white plastic breadboard in the Lab 0.1 write–up.

PB–10's. Many of you will use this course power supply breadboards with a "Model 1220 CA–1" power unit connected to a "PB–10" breadboard. These systems do not have power switches; just un–plug the power unit while you work on your circuit. Be careful to notice how the +5, ground, +12 and −12 volts rails are arranged on the connector to the PB–10. Furthermore, **halfway down each rail there is an open circuit which must be bridged by wires**; if a chip at the far end of the PB–10 doesn't seem to be getting any power, it probably isn't!

Bypassing. No power supply is perfect in the sense that only pure 5v and absolute 0v ground are represented on every extension of every wire of the power and ground system. Because of small resistances associated with the power supply and its wiring, sources of noise, especially transient voltage spikes generated by pulse circuits or by TTL gates changing state, can propagate through your system and upset your logic circuit, particularly at clock inputs on your sequential chips. Other noise may come from equipment turned off and on elsewhere in the lab, or 60 cycle noise from fluorescent lights, or reflections of voltages generated on long wires in your circuit, or your SONY Walkman.

To protect your circuit from these transient voltage spikes on the power supply lines, you can *bypass* or *decouple* the power supply by *placing capacitors directly from power to ground* at key places in your circuit, such as near clock pulse generation or clock pulse receiving chips. You can get 0.1 µF capacitors from the lab, and use them for bypass. These capacitors will *absorb* some of the current associated with the voltage transients. *Be aware of the possibility of bypass problems when troubleshooting your circuits! If a counter seems to skip values, or flip–flops seem to change state for no logical reason, bypass may be necessary!*

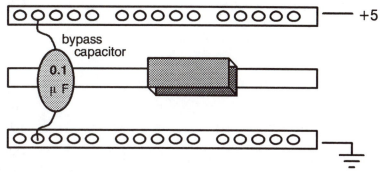

Digital Design Lab Manual

A capacitor is a charge storage element. Capacitors are discussed briefly in Chapter 8 Memory, with regard to dynamic RAM.

Power supply power. In the later labs, when you start adding many chips to you circuits, the total current required from the power supply will increase. For example, the 2901 chip uses 250 mA, the '181 chip uses 150 mA, and the EPROM about 100 mA. Your adaptor–style portable power supply is rated at 1000 mA @ 5v, but at levels above 500 mA, the voltage may dip below 4.75 v. If you have a circuit which continues to behave erratically after bypass or debouncing, use a voltmeter to check the actual +5–to–ground voltage across a few chips...make sure it's > 4.75 v. If your voltage level is giving your circuit a "brown–out", trouble shoot your circuit for current sinks (check your DIP switch) or change to one of the large higher current supplies in the lab.

Debouncing

Another source of unwanted pulses is mechanical switches, such as you have on your matrix keyboard. Suppose you press one of your keyboard buttons. Initially the two elements of the switch are separated or *open circuit*. Pressing the button will cause contact of the two elements. However, at the time of first contact, the elements may bounce away from each other on a microscopic scale of millisecond duration. Looking at the event with an oscilloscope you may see a series of pulses instead of the *one* pulse you desire. The figure below illustrates this problem and shows a method of *debouncing* **a 2–wire push button**.

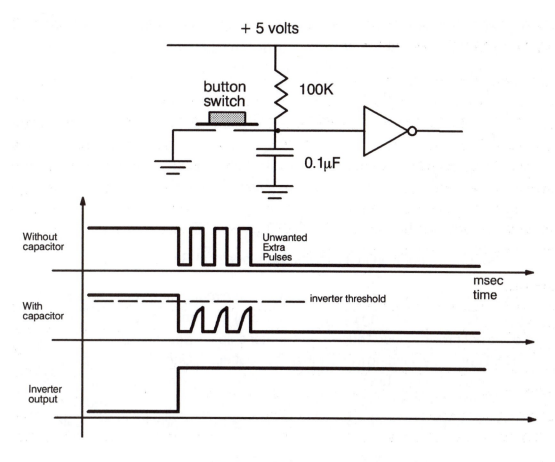

Debouncing

The solution idea here is similar to the solution of the bypass problem; a capacitor comes to our rescue. Use a *capacitor* to absorb some of the current associated with the unwanted pulse activity. In the figure we have a large resistance connected from the power supply to the gate input of an inverter. If there is no other voltage at the logic gate input, *the capacitor will remain charged to the power supply voltage*. If the gate input is grounded, as it can be with the press of a push button, the gate voltage will change *immediately* to 0v. (Why?). If mechanical bounce occurs and the contacts momentarily part, the capacitor will recharge with a time constant of RC. In the case of Figure 2, R X C = 10 milliseconds. If, well before those 10 milliseconds elapse, mechanical contact is made again, the gate voltage will again drop to 0 and be kept *below the threshold* which causes a change of state for the gate. Thus, the output of the gate *will remain* low in spite of small changes going on at the input, due to mechanical bounce. Of course, if the mechanical time constant is greater than 10 millisecond, a larger RC time constant will be needed.

You may first encounter the need for a debouncing circuit with the input buttons for the Lab 4 sequencer challenge. At that time you may want to use the capability of a **three termi-**

nal switch, (SPDT) instead of a two terminal push button. It's possible to de−bounce a three terminal switch with an RS latch, in a way that doesn't depend on an RC time constant. For the RS latch method, see the first part of Chpt. 5 in the text. Below is yet another way to de−bounce, using a 3−terminal switch such as you have in your kit, and a pair of inverters (say from 7414). The solution has the unpleasant feature that chip outputs are connected directly to ground.

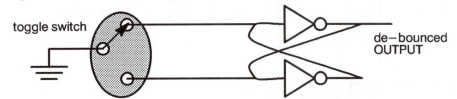

We saw this debouncing solution in a circuits "cookbook" at Radio Shack.

Along these same lines you may find odd results in circuits with clocks and counters. Two precautions (besides installing bypass capacitors) may help: (1) Sometimes the 555 clock chip does not provide good "edges" to counter chips expecting a rising edge clock; clean up the 555 output by sending it through a 7414 buffer. (2) Unconnected inputs on TTL chips float high in static cases, but can be easily changed by system transients in clocked circuits. Tie the "PRESET" and "CLEAR" pins high on TTL chip flip flops, if you don't want them to bounce around. Tie any other un−used inputs to appropriate logic levels.

"To a man with a hammer every problem looks like a nail."

Design, Troubleshooting & Frustration

Enough with the details of power supplies and logic probes...eventually they may the least of your problems during your encounters with digital design.

However well you organize your time, and are faithful to your schedule, you will still occasionally be frustrated by design or troubleshooting problems. With the following advice, we want to help you with your commitment to the course, so that halfway through the term, it has not become an anxiety crisis for you. Valium is not in your Bag−O−Chips!

Your first task with each challenge is **design**. Ideas may bubble forth only after you force yourself to read relevant material in the text, or study carefully the capabilities of pertinent chips in your kit. But suppose neither inspiration or forced study seems effective. Try this: Break the problem into smaller parts, each of which look manageable. For example, your circuit may require a sequencer. Design and build the sequencer; make sure it works. Your circuit may also have to respond to the commands of a particular button. Design and build that response and worry about the other parts later.

This piecemeal approach may lead you naturally to appreciate a method of design which circumvents the inspiration roadblock: *Over—engineering*. In digital circuit design, where the parts themselves are inexpensive, over—engineering has a respectable place in the designer's repertoire. Not to be confused with over—engineering, however, is the *tumor technique*. If your circuit gets bigger because of un—regulated growth, perform surgery. Likewise if you find yourself *gambling*, randomly disconnecting and reconnecting wires, or plugging chips into your circuit by intuition, say to someone, "Slap me if I do that again."

With regard to plugging more chips into your design, we remind you that **you can use only one of each chip in your kit. Your design will not be accepted if, for example you use two 7400 chips in a circuit.** Here's a tip on where you can find more combinatorial gates in your kit: the 74LS382. Look at the '382 data sheet to see how you can function—select so that you have, say, 4 more XOR's or 4 more AND gates; the '382 can even function as four 2→1 MUX's, in imitation of your 74157.

Your 2901 isn't as good as the '382 for combinatorial purposes, because the 2901 must have a register loaded before it can accept your inputs. The 2901, however, may come in handy supplying you with extra flip flops if you desperately need them.

Consider **Design.** Circuit design is a creative process, and in some ways can be difficult to teach, although much of what is written in the text can be thought of as design exercise examples. By learning about Boolean algebra, Karnaugh maps, synchronous counters, etc, you acquire the tools of design. To start a particular design, you first need well—stated specifications (which you get in the `Requirements` for each lab), and you need to *understand* the specifications. Usually the specifications state what the input and output should be, and leave as the design problem what goes in—between. What goes in—between will be, for you, a system of hardware chips. So you need to understand what your individual chips can do, in the same way you understand what different statements mean in a programming language.

Instead of worrying about the myriad possibilities of design for each challenge, let us assume you have achieved a circuit which, on paper or in simulation, looks as if it should work and yet does not give proper outputs after you have hooked it up and tested it. Of course if you really do have a design problem, don't hesitate to ask for help, or even re—read the recommended sections of the text. Don't be afraid to spend all day in the lab asking for help; that might be the shortest path in time to getting a design finished. Assume the design is implemented, now...

We will analyze the levels of frustration by dealing with **troubleshooting,** instead of the more nebulous design problem. First, in troubleshooting, calmly check your wiring. Are the power supply connections made properly? Are all the inputs to each gate accounted for?

Do all of the outputs go somewhere? Next, check the power supply. Are you getting the proper voltage? Is the polarity correct? If the power supply voltage has been reversed, all the chips in the circuit may be damaged. Does one chip seem like the culprit? Take it out and test it by itself; you may have a defective chip which you should exchange for a good one. **Don't throw the "bad" chip in the trash! Usually the chip isn't bad, it's you're wiring that's wrong! Give the chip to us and we'll save it to test later!** Are you having problems with clock signals? You may need to bypass or debounce as described in the Construction Guidelines. Test that "+5v" > 4.5, using a voltmeter.

You may find that an output pin is not behaving as you expect. Try pulling out all the wires that fanout from that pin, and see if the problem is still there. If the output pin now behaves properly, you have a **loading problem**. Re−connect the projections of the output pin, one by one, until the problem reappears...now you know what's causing the loading problem.

You may want to double−check interfaces between one kind of chip and another. For example, if you have an output from a gate driving a LED, the voltage across the LED in the "HIGH" state may be clamped lower than the HIGH logic levels required for other connections of that output. Or, you may have a CMOS chip fanning out to too many TTL chips. Or, you may have a TTL chip unable to reach input threshold voltage for a CMOS input. Is your problem intermittent? You may want to make sure that the wiring has been done in a neat manner, and you may wish to wiggle the wires in their breadboard socket holes to make sure there are no inadvertent open circuits. Unnecessarily long wires may cause reflection problems, especially in circuits with timing pulses. Bare wires may cause unwanted short circuits. Caution: don't bang your circuit board on the lab bench, or throw it against the wall...this will only further loosen wires.

Use the logic probe to test activity at various pins. If you have timing signals, you may want to sketch what you expect the timing waveforms to be and make sure that the proper events happen in the correct sequence by consulting the propagation delays listed in the data sheets. You may want to *single step* slowly through the states of your circuit. Or, if you examine timing waveforms with an oscilloscope or 1651A logic analyzer, you may discover one event is happening before or after it should according to the requirements of your circuit. You may have to introduce or remove delays from your circuits. If you wish, the 1651A can function as a 16−channel logic probe so you can watch many logic levels at once.

Suppose, however, that you have checked all these possibilities and your circuit still does not work. Do not give in to the usual behavioral impulses attendant with stage one frustration. Try another hour of redoubled effort checking your circuit's wiring again. You will develop a gnawing impression in stage one frustration that you are repeating the same tests over and over, to no beneficial effect. Your repeated acts, however, are an important form of learning.

"When you hear hoofbeats, think horses, not zebras."

Perhaps your bout with learning−by−repetition still leaves a circuit which does not meet requirements. Step away from the problem and sleep. We're not talking about a Rip Van Winkle solution here—just overnight; we are hoping that a subconscious integration of the paradoxes and dilemmas of your case will help dream therapy solve your problem.

Now suppose it is the next day, and the consolidation of sleep did not help. You stare blankly at your circuit. You are entering *state two frustration*. What next? Seek out the help of another student. You may ask someone who has already done the lab, or a student from last year's course, or you may have a sympathetic friend to whom you can explain out loud your situation and who may be able to spot an oversight. Resist the temptation to *borrow* someone's completed lab as a means to short circuit your frustration.

Maybe you can find no peer help for your problem. You feel yourself slipping into *stage three frustration*. You will now want to explain your problem to a TA. He may have a quick answer for you or may start with a discussion with you. He may want you to draw on paper your circuit design or set up some test which you both will study the results of. He may want to swap a couple of replacement chips in and out. If you have made a trivial error, he may point it out, and you will be free. If you are quite far from a solution, however, the TA may give you only general advice. You will remember that the lab challenges are not simply home-work problems that you are doing as practice for exams; the challenges are the basis of your grade itself, and as such, the TA will not spoonfeed an answer to you.

Suppose you implement the ideas of the TA. You may modify your circuit; you may even start over and build a new one. But, it is possible you will continue to fail. Things are grim now. You have entered *stage four frustration*. Why might this be? The TA may not have understood your design, or he may not have been willing to give you enough information for you to navigate out of your particular maze, or you may have simply been too depressed or too anxious to appreciate the advice.

In the depths of stage four frustration, you will now want to seek out The Professor for troubleshooting advice. Please have your circuit wired in a neat manner, with legible docu-mentation. The Professor will understand your circuit enough to make a judgment about it. He will tell you if your design can be made to work or if it is hopeless. He may suggest a new approach. Ask as many questions as you like. Be willing to endure a Socratic dialogue. Do not leave the meeting with The Professor unless you feel optimistic that further work will be profitable.

This advice about frustration will probably seem foolish as you proceed with the first few labs. We hope the advice will continue to be foolish as you proceed with the later labs. Our experience indicates, however, that the advanced labs may require significant attention to timing detail and knowledge of chips' capabilities. Frustration may lead you to think your circuit is haunted with gremlins, but EXOR stands for exclusive–OR, not exorcism.

A Zen perspective

Keep in mind your exclusive goal is to design, build (and answer FTQs about) a series of lab challenges. The challenges have been carefully selected to insure you learn the important concepts of digital and interface circuit design.

The weekly paper chase is gone– –you don't hand in this week's problem set at the same time you find out next week's assignment at the same time you get back last week's answers and corrections. Timed exams are gone—no more rush–rush–for–Orange–Crush anxiety while you cram information into your short term memory and hope you can stay interested in three hours of Trivial Pursuit. Beat–the–Clock cookbook labs are gone– –no more lab partners with the IQ of a shrub on one hand or the experience of Thomas Edison on the other; no more lab reports graded from 1 to 10 on neatness and precognition. When frustration strikes, meditate:

The real circuit you're troubleshooting is yourself.

> Buddha's way was quite different. At first he studied the Hindu practice of his time and area, and he practiced asceticism. But Buddha was not interested in the elements comprising human beings, nor in metaphysical theories of existence. He was more concerned about how he himself existed in this moment. That was his point. Bread is made from flour. How flour becomes bread when put in the oven was for Buddha the most important thing. How we become enlightened was his main interest. The enlightened person is some perfect, desirable character, for himself and for others. Buddha wanted to find out how human beings develop this ideal character—how various sages in the past became sages. In order to find out how dough became perfect bread, he made it over and over again, until he became quite successful. That was his practice.

Zen Mind, Beginner's Mind, page 56.

Digital Design Lab Manual

Soldering Tips

for your toggle, keyboard & potentiometer

1. Keep the Ungar soldering iron tip shiny & clean by wiping it on the WET sponge. *Keep the sponge soaked.*

2. DON'T "solder" the insulation...that will coat the tip with burned material, insulating the tip from its job and not allowing solder to flow on it. STRIP the insulation well away from the wire before starting to solder.

3. Pre–solder the wire before soldering to the device pin. Use the black–handled pliers & vise as a "third hand." You don't need to crimp the wire to the device...it'll just break off sooner.

4. Heat the metal work area until solder flows freely. The cooled solder should look smooth and shiny where the connection is made. Test your connection with a gentle tug.

5. UNPLUG the iron when you're finished. Don't worry, it'll heat up quickly for the next person.

Logic layout and simulation software
for the MacIntosh computer

FOR THE PACKAGES LISTED BELOW, THERE ARE ON–LINE AND PRINTED DOCUMENTATION.

MacBreadboard 1.16

If you like realism in computer graphics, you'll love MacBreadboard! MacBreadboard is required for Lab 0.1 and Lab 2SQ. In the 0.1 write–up there is more information about MacBreadboard. Select chips from a menu pulled down from the top bar. Connect inputs and outputs with colored wire by dragging the mouse. Remember to turn on the power supply to see your circuit in action, turn off the power supply to work on the circuit. There's a built–in logic probe when the circuit is on: just hold down the mouse button and see a red light if the "finger" points to a HI voltage. Unfortunately, only one breadboard is available for circuit building, so you may not be able to squeeze Lab 4 onto MacBreadboard. You're allowed to use any of the chips on the menu, if you want to give it a try.
If you want to try lab 3P with MacBreadboard, note that there are 74147 and 74148 priority decoders on the Chips menu.
Unconnected inputs should be tied to something, like ground or +5, to make sure they're what you think they should be! For example, in Lab 0.1, if you use the 283 adder, you may want to tie unused adder inputs to ground.

MacBreadboard 1.16 sometimes has bugs with regard to the adder chip 74LS283. You may want to re–wire parts of your circuit if you find your Lab 0.1 subtractor or Lab 2 squarer malfunctioning. As you construct a circuit, turn the power on occasionally to see if any err messages flash.

LogicWorks 2.5

LogicWorks from Capilano Computing in Vancouver, BC, allows for layout and simulation of combinational and clocked digital circuits. It has good features for connecting between inputs and outputs, and results in clean diagrams. The documentation book provides a good introduction to LogicWorks. You are welcome to use LogicWorks for Labs 4S, B, and 11, among others.

LogicWorks has various libraries under the DEVICES menu, including 7400 type counters and MUX's. LogicWorks hierarchical design feature is a little obscure, but comes under the Library options, where you can create your own Library.
To monitor points in the circuit go on the DEVICES menu and pick out a PROBE.
If "X" appears in the probe, trying "CLEAR TIMING" on the options menu.
You must use the SET and CLEAR inputs on a JK flip flop if you want an SR latch; you'll

actually have an S−bar, R−bar latch. Beware that the flip flop can hang up in a state where both Q and $\overline{Q}$ are 1; this seems to be a bug in LogicWorks.

By clicking on a device, you can change some of its parameters; for example, you can change the propagation delay through the device. To get timing to work, you have to use the "pencil" to name lines which will appear on the timing diagram. See a couple of the example circuits.

LogicWorks has two ways of deleting a connection. By highlighting a wire all wires connected to it are highlighted and CLEAR on the EDIT menu will remove them all. The ZAP lightning bolt will remove one branch at a time of a set of connected wires, and is a more precise delete tool.

You have various Library menus. Look under the DEMO LIB to find +5 and GND connections. The GATES Library has combinational gates; the GENERIC Library has various flip flops that you'll probably use for Lab 4S.

To make a circuit you create part of your own library, use the Development Editor menu and follow directions for naming your library, which will then appear under the Library sub−menu on the right. Modular design is extended by creating your own library.

You can use I/O Library **binary switch** to single step the clock for lab 4. Under the OP-TIONS menu release on CLEAR UNKNOWNS to assign values to all outputs at the start of a simulation.

If your Lab 4S circuit doesn't do anything and you've checked that flip flop R−S are tied HI, J−K inputs are not both LO and clock is active, make sure you've cleared unknowns AND that the simulation is in RUN or SLOW mode, not SINGLE STEP **(I.e. don't have on the icon of the man <u>sitting</u> in the chair).**

Another Lab 4S help from Capalino Computing: Try Karnaugh Works, in the Logic Works folder. No documentation for it, but you can enter your J and K maps in Karnaugh works to figure out the SOP or POS forms, with or without hazards.

Beige Bag V 3.0

Beige Bag is mainly the work of one person, Jon Engelbert, from Michigan. Beige Bag seems to have the look and feel of LogicWorks. It does use IEEE standard symbols for chips. Compared to LogicWorks, it seems to have a better chip library (74194, etc) and allows for easier hierarchical design: What you design can be packaged as a custom "chip" and used at a higher level. You are welcome to use Beige Bag for any appropriate lab.

DigLog

DigLog is a layout and simulation package written at Caltech; it is available on the Suns. If you know DigLog, you are allowed to use it for labs 4, B and 11. We won't be supporting DigLog in the current version of the course.

ViewLogic Corp. products

Form the ViewLogic Corp., PowerView and WorkView are a high—level layout systems which can download to FPGA place and route programs. You can learn more about Work-View in the field programmable gate array lab. WorkView is available off the Sun network.

CS31

FIRST Page
of DigLog
documentation.
See JD
for more.

GETTING STARTED

To start diglog, just type "diglog" and place the two windows somewhere on your screen. The first window will be your circuit board design space, and the second is a sort of terminal used occasionally for more complex commands.

To exit diglog, select "Exit" from the "Misc" menu, or type 'Q' in the primary screen and then answer "y" to the "Exit from program?" question you'll get in the other window.

USING THE PROGRAM

1. You control LOG mainly with the mouse, and also from the keyboard. It takes some time to get comfortable with the mouse in LOG, but it will soon become second nature. There are three basic mouse motions you need to learn:

2. TAP. Press and release the left button on a spot. This should feel like tapping a key on a keyboard. The spot you are tapping is indicated by the cursor on the screen, usually a small arrow.

3. PRESS/DRAG. Press down and hold the left button, move the cursor somewhere else, and release.

4. REST. Press the right button and release. This is used to cancel operations like drawing wires.

5. Some LOG functions appear right on the screen, so you can activate them just by tapping the word. Others are in "menus," which you get by pressing on one of the words Frills, Editing, Cursor, or Misc, then dragging to and releasing on the word you want. If you decide you didn't want the menu after all, just release on some other part of the screen.

6. There are also keyboard commands, though everything you really need as a novice can be found in on-screen menus. When you press a key for LOG, be sure the cursor is in one of the LOG windows (it doesn't matter which one). There are several features of the keyboard to notice:

7. SINGLE KEYS. Many commands appear on keys as well as menus, just for convenience. For example, you can press the letter "s" to do the same thing as SCOPE in the Misc menu.

8. <CNTRL>-C. Press the Control key and the "C" key together to exit from any mode you may find yourself in.

    SURVIVAL TIP #1: If you get lost and confused, press <CNTRL>-C
                      until you know where you are.

9. SPACE BAR. The space bar at most times means to refresh the screen. If the screen has gotten trashed by too much editing, press this key to clean it up. LOG will also silently clean up the screen if you stop editing for a few seconds.

Use of the Hewlett Packard 1651A Logic Analyzer

You've read *Feeling Comfortable with Logic Analyzers* and have watched a demonstration of the 1651A's use. And you may want to glance through the HP booklet with the logic analyzer, "Getting Started Guide." But now it's time to use the 1651 in the service of your own troubleshooting.

Getting started. The power switch for the machine is in back, next to where the power cord enters. The HP software disk must be in the disk drive, and for the first minute or so after power is turned on the disk drive will be active and loading; self–test operations will be going on. Eventually the `System Configuration` menu will appear on the screen. You can use the cursor wheel & select button to `Auto-scale` on the menu.

Pull out of the bag on top of the machine the 16 or so connectors for POD 1. <u>Notice how easy it is to push regular colored hookup wire into a POD connector hole, and then push the other end of the wire into your bread board.</u> *There are two endings to each cable; the one at the end of the flexible wire is signal, the stiffer one is ground; at least one ground wire should connect the logic analyzer to the circuit.* Push in eight different colored signal wires into connectors numbered 0–7. *Make sure the connector numbering corresponds to the cable numbering!* Now push the other ends of the wires into points in your circuit...voila, you have an 8 channel logic probe system! Just push the RUN button and the traces will display. If a trace is thick, it's logical 0, if it's thin, logical 1. If your signals change as a function of time you may see the changes on the time trace. If the logic analyzer says

`transitions remaining to PostStore`

it means you don't have *any* probes connected to changing signals. The logic analyzer wants to see at least one signal going through high–low–high transitions.

If the time–traces don't show up properly you'll probably need to adjust the SEC/DIV on the timing waveforms menu. Use the cursor & select controls to highlight the SEC/DIV box; then use the cursor to slow down the system, reading off the new SEC/DIV as you rotate the cursor. Press RUN again and see if your waveforms are switching back and forth in the display OK. If you select DELAY box and turn the cursor, you'll be able to move the waveforms around horizontally. This action simply reads a different section of the RAM where the waveforms are stored.

Grounding. If the waveforms you expect don't appear, and there seem to be puzzling glitches in the traces, CHECK THAT THERE IS ADEQUATE GROUND CONNECTION FROM THE LOGIC ANALYZER TO THE CIRCUIT. Normally this means that the ground from the pod goes the the circuit ground, but you may want to put additional ground wires in if the problems persists.

Basic Triggering. Here we assume you've got a clocked circuit, like lab 9, successive approximation 1–hot sequencer. In fact, there will be a demonstration of a pseudo random sequence generator, like the one described in text chapter 7. An oscillator will drive a 164 shift register; serial–in to the shift register will be XNOR of the two most significant bits of the 164 parallel output.

Refer to page 5–8 of the "Getting Started Guide." Go onto the TRACE menu. Select "binary" under the **base** menu, then go to "keyboard." Use the keyboard 0s and 1s to de-clare a pattern on which you want to logic analyzer to stop. Leave don't–care X's where you don't care, or where a probe isn't hooked up.

After you have the pattern option working, you might try out the "edge" feature. Once you select the EDGE box you'll see a row of 16 dots. Scoot the selector to the probe# (say a clock signal) you want to trigger on.
REMEMBER THAT PROBES ARE NUMBERED RIGHT TO LEFT! THE MSB PROBE IS ON THE LEFT!
Now as you repeatedly press SELECT you'll see the dot change to a ↓ then ↑ then up/down arrows then back to a dot. Normally you'd select ↑. Press RUN and see if the waveforms you need appear. A vertical dotted line will show where the trigger is. Again, you may need to adjust SEC/DIV and DELAY for the best view. Try DELAY and watch the trigger line scoot left and right.

If the SEC/DIV and "rate of" don't seem right,
try going back to the SYSTEM menu and selecting the AUTOSCALE feature again.

Be sure to store the "Getting Started Guide" back in the pouch on top of the logic analyzer when you finish.

**When Should I
Use a Scope?**

■ When you need to see small voltage excursions on your signals.
■ When you need high time-interval accuracy.

Generally, an oscilloscope is the instrument to use when you need high vertical or voltage resolution. To say it another way, if you need to see every little voltage excursion, like those shown below on the bottom waveform, you need a scope. Many scopes, including the new generation digitizing ones, can also provide very high time-interval resolution. That is, they can measure the time interval between two events with very high accuracy. Overall, an oscilloscope is to be used when you need parametric information.

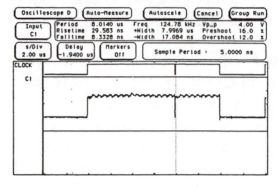

**When Should I Use
a Logic Analyzer?**

■ When you need to see lots of signals at once.
■ When you need to look at signals in your system the same way your hardware does.
■ When you need to trigger on a pattern of highs and lows on several lines and see the result.

Logic analyzers grew out of oscilloscopes. They present data in the same general way that a scope does; the horizontal axis is time, the vertical axis is voltage amplitude. But a logic analyzer does not provide as much voltage resolution or time interval accuracy as its cousin, the oscilloscope. It can capture and display eight or more signals at once, something that scopes cannot do. A logic analyzer reacts the same way as your logic circuit does when a single threshold is crossed by a signal in your system. It will recognize the signal to be either low or high. It can also trigger on patterns of highs and lows on these signals. So when do you use a logic analyzer? When you need to look at more lines than your oscilloscope can show you, provided you can live without ultra-precise time interval information. If you need to look at every little transition on the waveform, a logic analyzer is not a good choice (see the picture on the previous page). Incidentally, the display on the previous page was made with an HP 16500A which has both logic analyzer and digitizing scope channels.

Logic analyzers are particularly useful when looking at time relationships or data on a bus — e.g. a microprocessor address, data, or control bus. It can decode the information on microprocessor buses and present it in a meaningful form (more on this when we talk about state analyzers). Generally, when you are past the parametric stage of design, and are interested in timing relationships among many signals and need to trigger on patterns of logic highs and lows, the logic analyzer is a good choice.

Digital Design Lab Manual

EPROM addresses and the PROM programmer

Note: The PC file for the PROM data, **s163.dat,** can be made available to interested parties away from Brown University; contact me by e-mail.

Your erasable–programmable–read–only memory (EPROM) chip should have 28 pins, 8 of which are for output. See pinout in data sheets. In some labs you will use only the lower 4 bits of output. There are several different EPROMS in circulation for the Lab: 27512's, 2764's, 2764**A**'s and possibly 2716's. Your data sheets have the pinout for the 512's and 64's. The '512 is capable of addressing 64K locations 64K = 2^{16}, so it has 16 address pins, A_0 to A_{15}. The 2764 has 3 fewer address pins. In the applications for the following labs, pins A_{15} through A_{11} are always to be grounded. **If you have a 2764, then <u>pin 27</u> must be tied high for** READing; **on the '512 this pin is LOW during** READ.

Connect pins A_{10} to A_8 as follows, for the various labs

hex addr	A_{10}	A_9	A_8	
00XX	0	0	0	CPU Lab, 181 version
01XX	0	0	1	CPU Lab, 2901 version
02XX	0	1	0	Lab 6C
03XX	**0**	**1**	**1**	**Lab D**
04XX	1	0	0	Interrupt Lab
05XX	1	0	1	alternative Interrupt Lab

where XX indicates the lower 8 bits of EPROM address.

PROGRAMMING. The PROM's were programmed ("burned") with a PROM programmer PC card hardware and software from Needham Electronics, Sacramento, CA 916–924–8037 ($125). An old 286 AT machine was used. You can try the PROM programmer yourself. Before programming, the EPROM's were erased with ultra–violet light ("hard UV"—don't look at it!). The `ieprom` software from Needham is menu–driven and user friendly. Go to directory `ieprom` and run program `emp`. A menu will appear. Hit "5" to select the type of PROM you want to program (Don't insert the PROM until you have selected it's type from the menu; only insert or remove PROM's while the main menu shows.) The PROM should be inserted with its notch toward the socket lever, and its pins in the left–most slots (pins near the lever empty). Check that the PROM is erased with selection "2." Presumably the data to be programmed is in a file **s163.dat** in `ieprom` directory; load the file into the `ieprom` buffer with "8." If you need to edit the file, use "8." Type "0" or "1" to burn the PROM. Remove the PROM after return to the main menu.

EPROM: how does it work? Bits are stored as isolated charges on the gates of MOS transistors. The bits can be erased by placing the EPROM under ultraviolet light. Individual photons of UV are energetic enough to penetrate to the silicon surrounding the isolated gates, and create pathways for the gate to discharge. [Don't leave your EPROM's out in sunlight too long!] The gates can be written to by electrically filling up the gate with charge; a blank EPROM has all 1's; the writing process can only change 1's to 0's. Writing is done by raising one pin to a higher−than−5v signal, in a special PROM−programmer circuit, with is usually attached to a computer with an editor for storing the files to be written. The programming voltage goes to the select gate shown below. A computer program determines which addresses on the EPROM will be accessed. Take a look at the PROM programmer in the lab.

NEEDHAM SOFTWARE

See

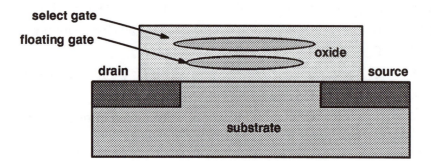

taken from Sedra & Smith, *Microelectronic Circuits, 3rd Edition*, Saunders, Phila. (1991), pages 967−70; Fig. 13.46.

In other words: Basically, the UV shines through a quartz window onto the insulating material surrounding floating gates in MOS transistors. The UV photons are energetic enough to knock charges out of the floating gate.

Programming PALs using PALASM on a PC
connected to a DATA I/O Box

How to get started with the PAL programmer.

In these notes we tell you how to program a 22V10 chip for either combinatorial or clocked sequential logic. You have a 22V10 in your kit. We will describe how to navigate around PALASM using the arrow keys instead of the mouse.

Read chapter 7 in *Digital Design from Zero to One* for more information about the 22V10. Also see page 2−245 of the green AMD PAL Databook for the "skinny DIP" circuit diagram and pinout. Basically the 22V10 PAL has 10 D−flip flops and a sum−of−products array which can form the excitation logic. The SOP outputs can bypass the flip flops and become direct combinatorial outputs if you like.

There are two volumes of documentation next to the PCs.
Chapter 2 of the *Getting Started* AMD book has useful information for a beginner.

1. Turn on the machine (switch at back right)
wait for the DOS prompt. Typing > cd \S163 sends you to our directory.
type > palasm
and wait for the AMD PALASM 4 logo to come on. Strike any key to continue.

2. You will be on the FILE menu
and one of the choices will be BEGIN NEW DESIGN.
Hit enter for that choice. Hit TAB after you land on a TEXT choice, and
you will be able to give an NEW FILE NAME filename.pds
the file name must end in .pds !!
Once you enter the filename and hit return, then hit F10 "form OK"

3. You will now pop to a menu system called PDS Declaration Statement
Use arrow down key to Author and type in your name.
Arrow down to DEVICE, where a menu will appear. Arrow down the menu
until you come to PAL22V10 and hit enter.
You're done with this menu. Hit F10 **twice** and ...

4. You go to the equation editor.
Use the arrow key to go down to PIN.
Now we will describe a way to make a 6−input AND−OR−INVERT gate (combinational)
Have the chip pinout handy as you declare what pins are what.
don't use the word NODE! just use word PIN for a 22V10.

Digital Design Lab Manual

Under the section PINS type

PIN 2 INa

PIN 3 INb

PIN 4 INc

PIN 5 INd

PIN 6 INe

PIN 7 INf

PIN 23 OUT

now under EQUATIONS type

OUT = /((INa*INb)+(INc*INd)+(INe*INf))

where / stands for invert, * is for AND and + is for OR

:+: is for XOR

5. When you're finished with the pins and equations, HIT ALT F

Yes, ALT F. You will see a menu. Choose SAVE and hit enter.

your file will be saved in the S163 directory.

HIT ALT F again and go to QUIT.

Now you're back in the main PALASM menu.

MORE: If you want to edit an existing file go to EDIT on the main PALASM menu.

6. Use the left arrow key to slide over to RUN.

Choose COMPILATION. accept default settings by hitting F10.

Now you wait while the compiler looks for errors in your PIN and EQUATION declarations.

If you've been very very good, there will be no errors.

If there are errors, you need to go back to the file and edit the pins and equations.

Use the EDIT menu on the top menu bar!

Otherwise the compiling process will generate two files, filename.jed

and filename.xpt the dot jed file will be downloaded to the programmer;

the dot xpt file has the fuse pattern in it, and you can, if you want to hand−tune your system

(don't for now...) go into the fuse pattern file and add your own Xs and Os.

If you get a compilation with no errors, hit the ESC key, which will return you to the main menu.

**ALL OF THE ABOVE EDITING COULD HAVE BEEN DONE ON A 386 or 486 computer IN THE LAB NOT CONNECTED TO THE PLD PROGRAMMER. BUT YOU WILL need to use a connected machine (or switch the mechanical multiplexer box) to access the DATA I/O programming box.

7. Slide over to DOWNLOAD and hit **enter.** your only option is GO.

Now you need to load the buffer in the programmer with your JED file.

Use the arrow keys to go to BUFFER LOAD then hit enter.

If you don't see your file on the menu list, make sure \S163*.jed is the directory path.

Use the arrow key to go to your file. Hit enter TWICE to download your file to the buffer.

Digital Design Lab Manual

8. Now slide the menu highlight over to DEVICE and choose PROGRAM on the second line. Use the arrow keys.

STOP! AT THIS POINT TURN ON THE PLD BOX AND SEE THE GREEN LIGHT. INSERT YOUR 22V10 WITH THE BOTTOM OF THE CHIP AT THE BOTTOM OF THE ZERO−FORCE−INSERTION SOCKET (LEVER ARM UP). MOVE THE LEVER ARM HORIZONTAL AND THE CHIP IS IN THE SOCKET. CHECK AGAIN THAT PIN ONE HAS LINED UP WITH THE 24−PIN MARKER LINE.

9. Hit enter for ACCEPT on the programming menu. After a few seconds the code will be successfully entered in the chip. Before the chip is programmed, it is electrically erased from its previous state. Pop the chip out by raising the lever arm, and go test your chip in a breadboard! Don't forget PIN 24 is Vcc and PIN 12 is GROUND.

WAIT! HOW DO YOU KNOW WHICH PIN DOES WHAT? (You need documentation!) Either you printed out your editor file, or you drew a pinout on a piece of paper.

10. INFORMATION ABOUT FSM EQUATIONS.

As you can tell from reading chapter 2 of *Getting Started*, PALASM knows that you want "registered" outputs by looking for := assignment statements in the equation section.

If you want to use the flip flops in the 22V10 (and you'll need to for all the FSM design problems) note from the pinout that PIN 1 is CLK !

PIN 13 is 3−state output enable, if you want that, too.

At any rate, suppose you typed in

PIN 1 CLK
PIN 2 INP
PIN 22 Q0
PIN 23 Q1

equations...
Q0 := INP*/Q0
Q1 := Q0

you will be telling PALASM that the flip flops on pins 22 and 23 are to be called Q0 and Q1, and that their D inputs are assigned as given in the Q0 and Q1 equations. It will be some kind of 2−bit counter.

Try going through this PAL programming process once ortwice with your 22V10.
Because it has so much functionality, the 22V10can be programmed
to do almost anything you want in the course .
Chapter 2 of the AMD documentation has more detail.
For example, see what happens when you type "Moore machine" in your file declaration!

You can examine successful PALASM files in the S163 directory.

Digital Design Lab Manual

THE LAB CHALLENGES: −1 TO 13₁₆

Lab Minus One

−1   Destroy a Display

Requirement: Burn out a segment of your three-digit seven-segment common-cathode multiplexed display, HP 7433.

(replacement cost = $9, yikes!)

Discussion: In keeping with the concept of negative numbers, you receive credit for lab minus one by **not** doing it. Thus, if you **do** burn out a segment, you **won't** receive credit for this lab. Before placing the HP 7433 display chip in your kit we tested it to make sure all it's segments light*. You automatically have credit for Lab Minus One when you receive your kit.

How can you burn out a segment? *By allowing too much current to pass through the segment.* How much is too much? The HP data sheet states that peak current per segment = 50mA. According to Ohm's Law,

$$V = I \times R = 5\, volts = 50 \times 10^{-3} \times R$$

if we're using a 5 v supply.

So if $R < \dfrac{5}{50 \times 10^{-3}} = 100\Omega$ we may burn out a display segment.

This calculation assumes the voltage is applied to a *forward biased* diode (see figure below). When you are probing pairs of pins to determine the pinout of the display you will be safe if you use a 100Ω (brown−black−brown) resistor in series with +5v and ground, the other probe. Labelled resistors can be found in drawers in the lab.

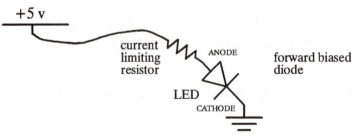

On the other hand, If you place *too much* resistance in series with a segment (> 1KΩ) the segment will be too dim for good visibility.

*We have not tested <u>all</u> the chips in your kit, however; so if a circuit does not work, one possibility to consider is a bad or semi−bad chip!

Each segment is a light−emitting diode (LED), with a visible* output at 656nm red. The I−V plot of a diode is shown in Fig. ii.

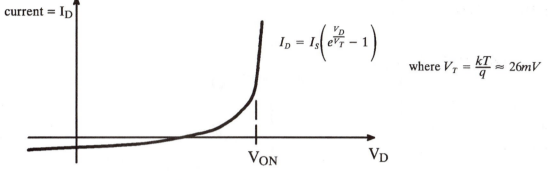

$$I_D = I_S\left(e^{\frac{V_D}{V_T}} - 1\right)$$

where $V_T = \dfrac{kT}{q} \approx 26mV$

Figure ii: Diode I−V plot

Later, after you have determined which pins connect to the segment anodes (and which connect to the common digit cathodes) you will be safe using a 7448 or DS8856 decoder−driver chip to drive the display *with no intervening resistors* because those chips limit current output internally.

A diode does not obey Ohm's law! It has an exponential (non−linear) I−V relationship; the relationship is *temperature−sensitive,* a fact you may utilize in a temperature controller. For a regular p−n junction silicon diode, $V_{ON} \approx 0.7v$;
for our LED's $V_{ON} \approx 1.7v$. See section on D−A converters and op amps for a rectifier circuit which creates an "ideal" diode, and for another circuit which uses the exponential relationship to create a logrithmic compression amplifier.

If a diode is placed from the output of a logic chip to ground, the chip output will be *clamped* to V_{ON} when the chip output is driven to a *HI* state. A value of 1.7 volts is *less than the minimum high output* expected by other chip inputs. Loading chip outputs with LED's can be a source of problems *unless* a 100Ω resistor is placed in series with the diode to raise the effective clamp voltage.

What does it mean that your display is a **common cathode** device? It means that all the *cathode* ends of the seven segment diodes (and decimal point) are connected together at *one* output pin, which normally should have a pathway to ground (perhaps through a transistor, if the digits are to be multiplexed in their display). See figure below.

---

* Electrons crossing the forward−biased p−n semiconductor junction give up energy in the form of photons, which, by the formula E = hν, end up with a frequency ν which is visible to the human eye. Remember, photons can be considered particles or waves.

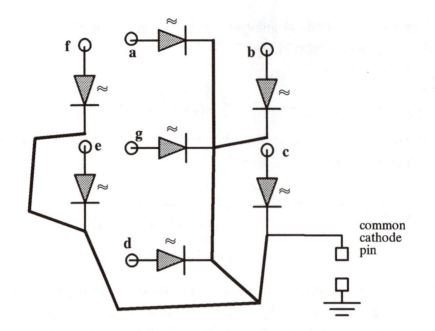

Figure iii: Common cathode connections for one digit of LED

The common cathode pin must have a pathway to ground for the segments of the digit to light up.

What is a **multiplexed** display? It is one in which the anodes for each corresponding pair of segment anodes (eight pair in all, counting the decimal point) are connected together. See figure below for a 3–digit display.

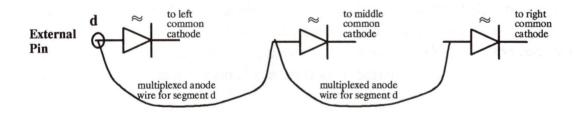

Three digit segment multiplexing

The signals for a left, middle and right digit segment must share a common pin. The segment information for two or three digits must be *multiplexed* (must share, in the time domain, a common wire).

Bottom–line advice for not doing lab −1 when you're trying to do lab 1: place a 100Ω resistor in series with the +5 volt probe you use to test pairs of pins on the 7433 display chip. The 100Ω resistor won't be needed when you finally figure out how to connect the 7433 anodes to a driver like the 7448.

So much for discussion about your 7−segment display. The stand−alone light emitting diodes (LED's) in your kit must also be protected from too much current, either with a current limiting resistor (100Ω), or by a chip output. Placing these diodes, forward biased directly across +5v to ground, will burn them out. (If you place a diode in a circuit *backwards,* it just won't light up, but it won't burn out, either.)

Your 2N4401 npn transistor has a base−emitter np junction which also must be protected by a current−limiting resistor. See figure.

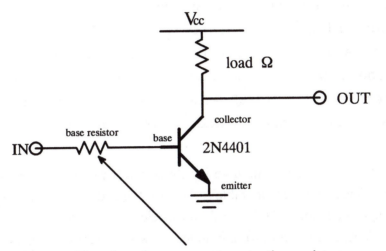

Figure v: Transistor base current protection resistor

The base resistor should be 1KΩ or larger. The load resistor can be considerably smaller, 100Ω or maybe less. More later in Lab 5, on calculating load resistors.

Good luck **not** doing lab −1!

Lab 0.1

0.1   Two-bit Subtractor

Requirements: Using the MacBreadboard simulator, design and build a circuit which can subtract two 2-bit numbers, R-S. Both R and S will be unsigned numbers. The circuit must also accept a "borrow-in" input. The output will be two DIFFERENCE bits and one BORROW-OUT bit; the outputs can be displayed as three "OUTPUT LEDs" on the MacBreadboard graphic. Since the output can be negative, it may appear as a 3-bit 2's complement result. The FIVE inputs can come from the E-L "DIP" switches at the top of the breadboard graphic.Expect for the 74283 adder, you can use only one each of the various chips on the MacBreadboard "Chips" menu in your design.

Discussion: Your 2-bit problem has 5 inputs, so the truth table has $2^5 = 32$ lines and 3 outputs per line. The complete truth table is shown at the end of this write-up. When we ask you a fault tolerance question (FTQ), you should circle on the truth table where mistakes will occur after the selected wire is removed. Practice a few subtraction problems, especially with borrow input, or with S > R, to get a feel for binary subtraction.

"Borrow in" and "borrow out" can be confusing terms. What's being computed here is $R - S - B_{IN}$. Therefore borrow-in is perhaps better thought of as "borrow-from," because it represents a taking away from the left column offering a 1 bit, to be subtracted from the R bit. And borrow-out might be thought of as "borrow-request," because it tells the next column to the left that a borrow bit is needed. See the modular method below, where one-bit full subtractors are chained together for a 2-bit solution.

A **One Bit Full Subtractor** (1BFS) truth table is shown below, along with a graphic symbol to the right.

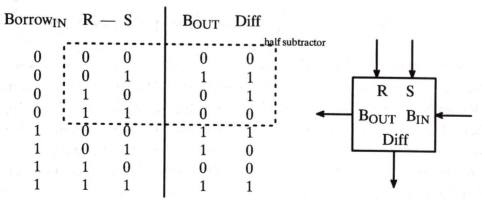

Borrow$_{IN}$	R	— S	B$_{OUT}$	Diff
0	0	0	0	0
0	0	1	1	1
0	1	0	0	1
0	1	1	0	0
1	0	0	1	1
1	0	1	1	0
1	1	0	0	0
1	1	1	1	1

Like with the one bit full **adder** sum output, DIFF can be computed efficiently with 2 XOR gates. And, like the one−bit full adder built from two half adders, the 1BFS can be built from two half subtractors. The **half subtractor** will realize the 2−in, 2−out, truth table dotted above, and will look like:

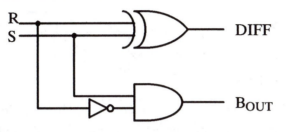

Compare the half subtractor to the half adder in text Chapter 1, and try to figure out how two half subtractors can be combined for a full subtractor. XOR gates can be used for the **DIFF** output. Once you have a full subtractor built, combine it with another full subtractor, as shown below.

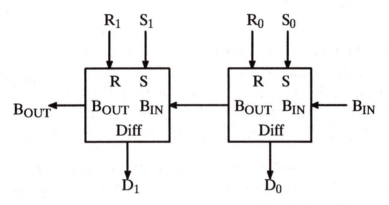

$R_1R_0 - S_1S_0 - B_{IN}$ is computed.

Multiplexers for B_{OUT}: In chapter 4 of the text multiplexers are discussed. You can use an to realize <u>any</u> 3−input truth table. Think about using a multiplexer to realize B_{OUT} of a one bit full subtractor. An 8→1 MUX is available on MacBreadboard. *Another chip to consider: the AND−OR−INVERT, which can realize the 1−bit B_{OUT} in one chip.*

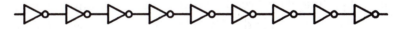

2's complement method for subtracting. As you can see in Chapter 1 of the text, subtraction can be done by converting the subtrahend to a 2's complement code negative number then using adder hardware. Since your problem is $R - S - B_{IN}$, re−write as $R - (S + B_{IN})$ to see that $S+B_{IN}$ is the term to be subtracted. To convert $S+B_{IN}$ to a negative number, invert it and increment the result. If S=11 and B_{IN}=1 then $S+B_{IN}$ = 100, a 3−bit number. To accommodate a 3−bit number, 4 bits of 2C code is required. The diagram below shows how 3 adders can accomplish the result.

Digital Design Lab Manual

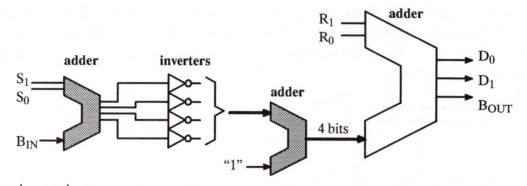

The 2nd and 3rd adders can be combined by using carry–in to increment. The three least significant bits out of the last adder will be the correct answer, with the most significant bit B_{OUT}.

Sum of products. Chapter 2 of the text introduces you to a 2–level AND–to–OR method for realizing any truth table. Trying to realize all three columns of the truth table by sum of products is likely to result in a design which is too big for MacBreadboard. Take note that the difference columns can be realized by XOR gates, and concentrate on the B_{OUT} column for the straight SOP design. As shown in text chapter 3, you can more easily minimize the B_{OUT} design by drawing out the I/O relationship on a Karnaugh map (in this case a 5–input map!).

About MacBreadboard. MacBreadboard 1.16 will be on the server at the CIT and on Macs in room 340 and 450. For the CIT, find out the login and password at the beginning of class. Lab 0.1 can be checked off in the lab or in the CIT. MacBreadboard shows a faithful graphic rendition of the Global Specialties EXP 300 solderless breadboard, that you'll receive in your kit. On the screen the breadboard is surrounded by input switches and output LEDs (light–emitting diodes). See printout of MacBreadboard screen at the end of this write–up. Go to the **Chips** menu and select a 7400 by dragging the mouse down and releasing. You'll see a 7400 chip pop up, straddling the central canal of the breadboard. You can move the chip to other positions before connecting it to power and ground. Double–click on the chip to see its internal pinout. Notice that the chip on the breadboard inserts into the E and F rows. Each A–B–C–D–E and F–G–H–I–J five hole column is internally connected. For example, pin 14 is connected to row E, and is therefore in contact with holes A, B, C, & D of its column. The X and Y rows at the top and bottom of the breadboard are each internally connected. You need to run a wire from the +5 area to row X and from the GND area to row Y. On most chips (but not the 7476, for example) the top left pin (14?) must be connected to the +5 row and the bottom right pin must be connected to the GND row.

Click and drag to route wires. The color menu allows you to use length, node, or "custom" to choose wire colors. To delete a wire, select by clicking (the wire will blink) then use the standard mac keyboard operation <⌘x> to "cut" the wire. You can also select CUT WIRE under the Edit menu. You might want to be careful routing wires, so your wires stay visible, and don't land on top of each other too often!

Digital Design Lab Manual

YOU CAN EDIT YOUR MacBreadboard CIRCUIT ONLY WHEN THE POWER SWITCH IS OFF!

Once you have something working on your MacBreadboard circuit, turn it on and test it. You have a built−in logic probe when the simulator is powered on. Hold down the mouse button and a red light will come on when the "finger" is pointing at a logical HI point, and will be black if the finger is on a logical LO or on an unconnected hole. It seems that unconnected inputs stay low on M^{C}BB.

As you build up your circuit (especially when using '283 adders) occasionally turn on the power button to see if you get any error messages; "feedback loop" error can be particularly frustrating; you may need to pull out wires until the error message goes away. You may want to build your circuit modularly at any rate, so that after you've done some work, you can test a sub−circuit.

For Lab 0.1 you can use any of the chips on the CHIPS menu, but you can use any particular chip only once—*Except for the 74283 adder, which you can use as many times as it will fit on the breadboard.* You do have two different quad XOR chips, the 7486 and the 74386. Only 8 of the M^{C}BB chips will be in the hardware kit you fill out after completing Lab 0.1. Two of the handiest chips may be 7400 (NAND) and 7486 (XOR), which are further described in the first few pages of the data sheets. Notice that pin 14 of each chip must be connected to +5v and pin 7 of each chip must be connected to ground.

The 74LS283 4−bit adder. Not shown on the MacBreadboard pinout for the '283: pin 16 is for +5 V power, and pin 8 is to be grounded!

Normally an unconnected TTL input will float high, but in MacBreadboard unconnected inputs seem to stay low. *For Lab 0.1 assume that an unconnected M^{C}BB input is at logical LO. This assumption may be important in answering your FTQ. In fact you may want to connect unused inputs to either HI or LO just so you're sure what they are.*

Here is the 2−bit subtraction truth table, for $R - S - B_{IN}$
Can you find any errors? Is B_{OUT} like the sign bit for 3−bit 2's complement code?

B_{IN}	R_1	R_0	S_1	S_0	B_{OUT}	D_1	D_0
0	0	0	0	0	0	0	0
0	0	0	0	1	1	1	1
0	0	0	1	0	1	1	0
0	0	0	1	1	1	0	1
0	0	1	0	0	0	0	1
0	0	1	0	1	0	0	0
0	0	1	1	0	1	1	1
0	0	1	1	1	1	1	0
0	1	0	0	0	0	1	0
0	1	0	0	1	0	0	1
0	1	0	1	0	0	0	0
0	1	0	1	1	1	1	1
0	1	1	0	0	0	1	1
0	1	1	0	1	0	1	0
0	1	1	1	0	0	0	1
0	1	1	1	1	0	0	0
1	0	0	0	0	1	1	1
1	0	0	0	1	1	1	0
1	0	0	1	0	1	0	1
1	0	0	1	1	1	0	0
1	0	1	0	0	0	0	0
1	0	1	0	1	1	1	1
1	0	1	1	0	1	1	0
1	0	1	1	1	1	0	1
1	1	0	0	0	0	0	1
1	1	0	0	1	0	0	0
1	1	0	1	0	1	1	1
1	1	0	1	1	1	1	0
1	1	1	0	0	0	1	0
1	1	1	0	1	0	0	1
1	1	1	1	0	0	0	0
1	1	1	1	1	1	1	1

Lab Zero

0   One Bit Full Adder

Requirements: Design and build a one bit full adder using only one 7400 (NAND) chip and one 7486 (XOR) chip for logic. The two outputs--"sum" and "carry out"--must be displayed with two LED's. The three inputs can be sent along three wires connected manually to +5v or to ground (for "1" or "0" inputs, respectively).

Discussion: The One Bit Full Adder truth table is shown below.

Carry$_{IN}$	B	A	SUM	Carry$_{OUT}$
0	0	0	0	0
0	0	1	1	0
0	1	0	1	0
0	1	1	0	1
1	0	0	1	0
1	0	1	0	1
1	1	0	0	1
1	1	1	1	1

Find the pinouts of 7400 and 7486 in the first few pages of the data sheets, or from a TTL Databook. Notice that pin 14 of each chip must be connected to +5v and pin 7 of each chip must be connected to ground. Realization of truth tables is the topic of *Digital Design from Zero to One* chpt. 2.

Lab Zero is a great way to learn about MacBreadboard software, but you can just as easily do Lab Zero with real chips and wires and switches and LEDs.

The holes in EXP–300 breadboard are connected as shown in the xerox on the next page. All the holes in top row "X" are connected together, as are all the holes in the bottom row "Y." Normally you run a wire from +5 volts on the power supply to "X," and another wire from Ground to "Y." Straddle a chip across the trough in the middle of the board, and press its pins into holes in rows "E" and "F." Each set of A–E holes is connected together, as is each set of F–J holes. Thus each pin from the chip is accessible through four other holes, either A–D or G–J.

For example, if you've pressed your 14 pin 7400 chip into columns 1–7, then you can run a wire from a hole in row "X" to hole A1 and you will have provided your chip with +5 v. Likewise a wire from a hole in row "Y" to hole J7 will ground your chip.

Note the orientation of pin 1 on the chip in the xerox.

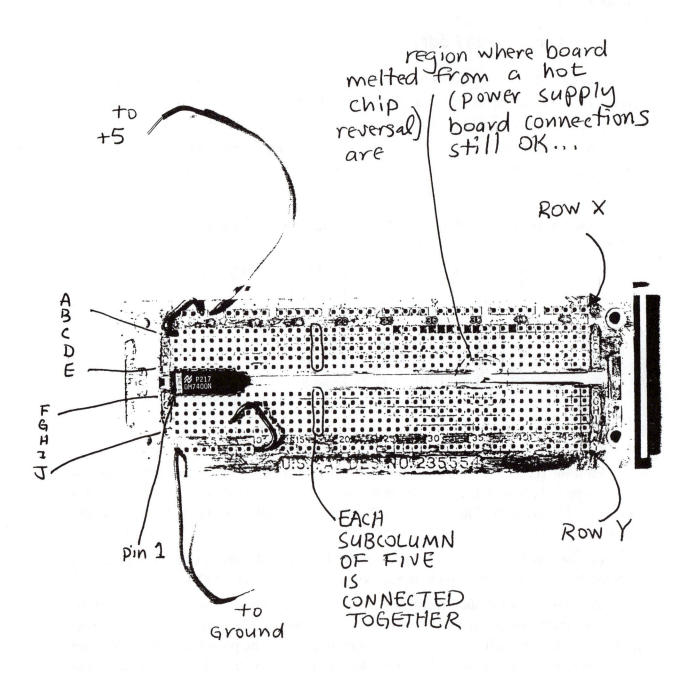

to
+5

region where board
melted from a hot
chip (power supply
reversal) board connections
are still OK...

Row X

A
B
C
D
E

P217
DM7400N

F
G
H
J

Pin 1

to
Ground

EACH
SUBCOLUMN
OF FIVE
IS
CONNECTED
TOGETHER

Row Y

Lab One

1   Multiplexed Display

Requirements: With your toggle switch in position A, display 23 on your pink HP 7433. For position B, display 59. Each display must be flicker-free. The HP 7433 has three digits; if you make a 3-digit switched display of 123 & 759 you won't have to answer an FTQ.

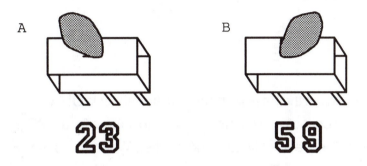

Toggle positions & resulting displays

8164
extra digits

23 59 IS THE MAXIMUM HOUR:MIN READING ON A 24 HOUR CLOCK

(You can use the soldering iron in the lab to connect ≈ 22 gauge hook−up wire to the three pins of the toggle switch. Read "Soldering Tips" for more information about proper use of the Weller soldering iron.)

Discussion: The pin−out of the 7433 display is NOT in your data sheets, so the first thing to do is determine the 7433 pinout. (Consult Lab Minus One for background and warning.) You'll want to probe pairs of 7433 display pins with a ground wire and a +5v−**in−series−with−100Ω**−resistor + wire. You'll soon discover which pins are the common cathodes. For the three digits, find out which seven pins control the seven segment anodes, which one controls the decimal point, and which pins have no connection (NC). Remember—don't do lab minus 1 while you're finding out how your display works! Have the **100Ω**−resistor in series with the +5v power! When you finally hook up the 7433 to a display driver chip, the 100Ω won't be necessary.

100Ω resistors are available from the bins in the lab.

In order to make the display flicker−free, you'll need to use a pulse generator chip, such as the 555, to create a back−and−forth changing signal which will select first one digit and then the other. We'll show you a "recipe" for the 555 later in the lab.

Understand how an npn transistor can be used as a **switch** to control current from common cathode to ground.

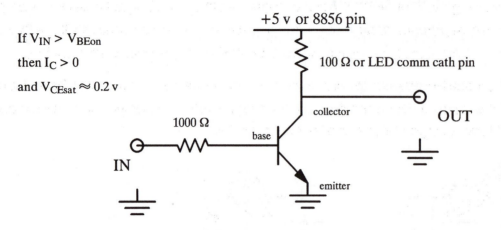

If $V_{IN} > V_{BEon}$

then $I_C > 0$

and $V_{CEsat} \approx 0.2$ v

1000 Ω

IN

+5 v or 8856 pin

100 Ω or LED comm cath pin

collector

OUT

base

emitter

In common–emitter configuration, when the base is "high," the transistor is ON. When the transistor is ON current can flow from collector to emitter (or drain to source for an MOS transistor) because of a low resistance between collector and emitter. When the base is **low**, the transistor is OFF and no current flows. The base–emitter pn junction is a diode and so must be protected from excess current (put a resistor in series with the base!).

Note that the transistor as a switch, with emitter grounded, functions as an **inverter**. When input (the voltage applied to base resistor) is high, output (collector voltage) is **low** because of the low resistance from ground to the collector! Conversely, when the input is low, the collector is held to a voltage closer to +5v (high) because the load = collector resistance is relatively less than the now–greater collector–to–emitter resistance to ground! You'll read more about this in the supplemental chapter on chip characteristics.

You have two discrete transistors in your kit: a 2N4401 npn bipolar and a VN40AD n–channel VMOS. Both can be used to control current flow from digits of the display. See the data sheets for their pinouts. Other transistors in your kit, including the output transistors buried in the 7406 or 555 chips, can also be used.

You want a display that is flicker–free for human perception. This means a rate of switching back and forth between the digit–controlling transistors greater than 50 Hz. In one phase the left digit will be on for a few milliseconds while the right is off, then the right is on, while the left is off...To bring in the two digit's worth of information, you'll want to use a **multiplexer,** discussed in text–Chapter 4 (Hey, it's not called Multiplexed Display Lab for nothing). But to control the display device itself, you may need **de**–multiplexing...again look in Chapter 4. The pulse generator will control HP display digit selection, and control which number will be displayed on the selected digit.

The output transistor of the 555 can "sink" the current from one digit, if you would like to replace a discrete transistor. Once you are able to switch the two digits off and on (de−multiplex the pulse generator) you will need to coordinate that switching action with the proper signals for the segments. You can drive the segments directly with your 7448 or 8856 decoder driver. You will need to *multiplex* the four 8856 <u>inputs</u> with appropriate chips.

Finally, make the output of your toggle switch influence the responses of the multiplexing chip. The figure below illustrates how the toggle switch pins work. You'll need a combinational logic design that the middle switch pin feeds into.

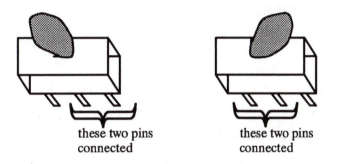

these two pins
connected

these two pins
connected

Toggle switch positions

You have three multiplexers (7415X), in your kit; look them over and decide which to use. You shouldn't need to use the deMUX chip in the two−digit problem. Again, multiplexers and demultiplexers are discussed in Chapter 4 of the text.

Possible FTQ (fault tolerance question): <u>Draw out</u> on paper how to make your display show <u>three</u> <u>different</u> numbers on your three digit display. Account for a flicker-free display. In figuring out this problem, you'll be on the road to solving Lab 4K, the keyboard encoding lab.

1 The 555 Timer

with information at end of file about 654 VCO chip

1.1 555 chip

In the 555 timer chip two analog comparators provide input to an SR latch. The latch output controls whether or not an open–collector transistor is turned on. By attaching an RC circuit to the open collector, and sending the collector voltage back to the input, an oscillator or 1–shot can be constructed.

reference: Walter G. Jung, *IC Timer Cookbook, 2nd Edition,* (1983)
Sams, 4300 W. 62nd St., Indianapolis, IN 46268 USA.

1.1.1 Relaxation Oscillator
Consider an RC circuit

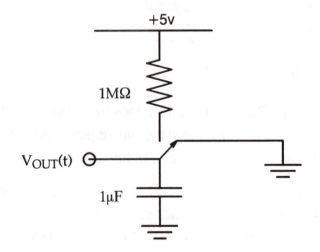

This circuit starts out with the switch connected to ground, as shown. The capacitor is discharged. What will be the voltage $V_{OUT}(t)$ as a function of time, after switch S is thrown from ground to +5? Of course $V_{out}(t)$ starts at 0 = ground. Think of the capacitor acting as a reservoir, filling with charge (see §1 for discussion of resistors and capacitors); how long will the "filling" take? The answer is sketched below, after the switch has been moved from ground to resistor. The "emptying" of the capacitor, after switching back to ground, will be instantaneous because there will be zero resistance on the ideal switch pathway to ground.
Recalling that $1M\Omega = 10^6$ ohms and $1\mu F = 10^{-6}$ farads we have $R{\cdot}C = 1$ sec,
[Ohms·Farads has units of seconds.] the time constant for this circuit.
The equation of the line is $V_{OUT}(t) = 5 \cdot (1-e^{-t})$, where e is the base of the natural logarithms, 2.7183... You don't need to worry about how this equation is derived; you may have seen the derivation in a sophomore–level circuits course for engineers.

Digital Design Lab Manual

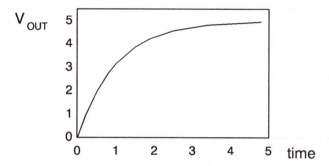

When t = τ = RC, then V$_{OUT}$ has climbed to within 1/e of its asymptotic value 5v. The important point here: The capacitor takes some time to charge up through resistor R, and we can use that time to control the rate of change of an oscillator's frequency.

see for example J. Nilsson, *Electric Circuits, 4th ed.* Addison−Wesley (1992)

To use the charging RC circuit in an oscillator we need another element: The volt-age−sensitive switch. As we saw in Chapter 1,, "voltage−sensitive switch" can be another name for transistor. Here, is an npn transistor in an inverting switch circuit:

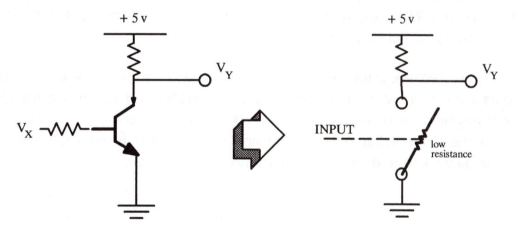

When V$_x$ is HIGH, then "the switch is closed."
We can incorporate the transistor in the next stage of our oscillator design by letting the capacitor's path to ground pass through the transistor:

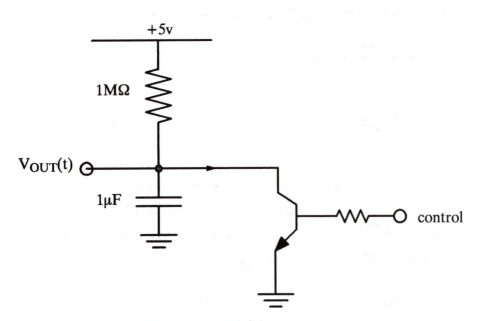

Now when the control voltage is HIGH the capacitor will be (virtually) grounded, and when the control voltage is LOW the capacitor will charge up to the 5v level with a time constant of 1 sec. What voltage should go to the control pin? You can see where we're headed when you consider that, if Vout is high, the transistor will turn ON and the capacitor will discharge and Vout will go LOW and the transistor will turn OFF and the capacitor will start charging up again, and so on...an oscillator!

   If the control voltage is low then the switch is open and the output voltage Vout heads toward its asymptotic value +5. At this point we haven't hooked up the switch's control voltage to anything... Now here's the idea: Feed back Vout to become the control voltage. Then when the control voltage exceeds the threshold voltage of the switch, the capacitor will discharge back to zero and so on, repeating as an oscillator...

Here we have attached V_{OUT} directly to the control pin, as shown:

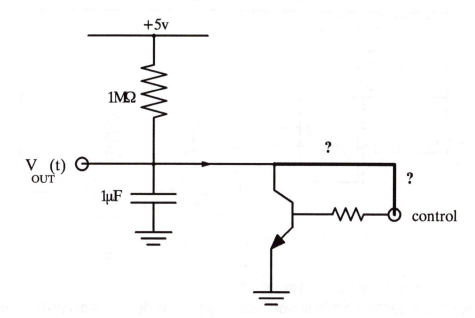

Yes, this circuit will oscillate, but not in a way useful for us.
[SHOW REAL RESULTS FOR 2N4401 XSISTOR...SCAN PHOTO OF 'SCOPE FACE...]
If we imagine the transistor acting as a nearly ideal switch, with a threshold control voltage θ for changing from OFF to ON, then, after starting at initial condition of 0, the output will chatter like:

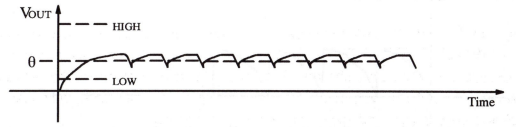

   The problem: V_{OUT} will switch back and forth between two levels near θ; V_{OUT} will not reach logic voltage levels of LOW and HIGH. As soon as θ is crossed in one direction or another, the transistor will switch back as fast as it can, and reverse the change of V_{OUT}. What we need is a way to make the transistor stay ON or OFF long enough to reach our digital logic levels. We can accomplish this with hysteresis, or with an RS flip flop, as shown below.

Digital Design Lab Manual

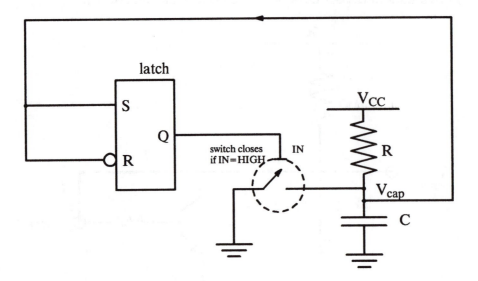

Here the transistor is shown as a switch. The flip flop will SET only when V_{cap} charges up to logical 1, then the switch will flip on, instantly grounding and discharging the capacitor, sending V_{cap} to logical 0. RESET on the flip flop will occur at that point, and the switch will open, allowing the capacitor to charge back to logical 1, with a time constant of RC. V_{cap} will have a waveform like

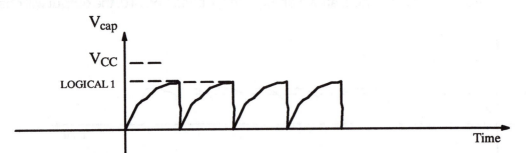

Discharging a capacitor to ground through a transistor, without any regulation by a resistor, may cause too much current to flow through the transistor.

Oscillating latch: Hook Q up to R, $\overline{Q}$ up to S.

1 .1 .2 The 555 timer chip as an oscillator

The next design shows this idea extended, with a transistor as a switch, a resistor to regulate discharge, and level detectors on the inputs of the RS flip flop.

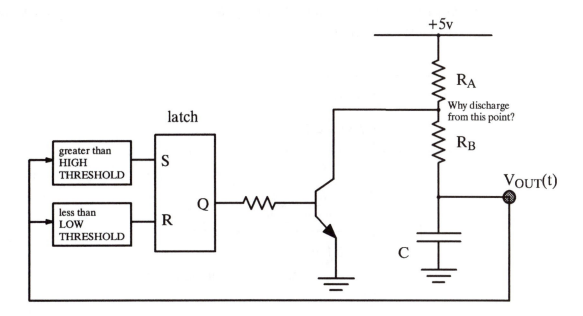

Follow this reasoning: When high threshold from **V**OUT is detected, then Q goes high and the transistor turns ON and the capacitor discharges through the transistor via resistor R$_B$. Even after V$_{OUT}$ drops below high threshold, the flip flop output Q will stay high, until the discharge takes V$_{OUT}$ below low threshold, at which time RESET will become HIGH and Q will go low and the transistor will go OFF and the capacitor will start to charge through R$_A$ + R$_B$ until V$_{OUT}$ exceeds high threshold and the process starts over... Let's show this process with a timing diagram:

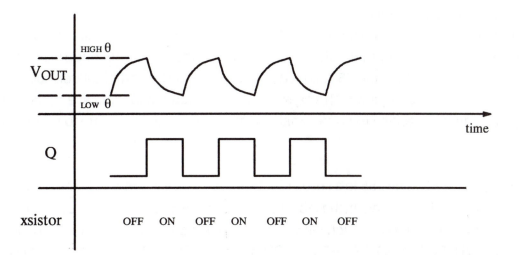

Notice that second resistor, R$_B$, slows the rate of discharge; in the timing diagram above we've set R$_B$ >> R$_A$, so charging and discharging will have nearly the same time constant. Now we've got our oscillator, with output Q going between logic HIGH and LOW, and a period determined by C, R$_B$ and R$_A$. [THIS, BY THE WAY, IS THE BASIC DESIGN OF THE 555 TIMER

CHIP, USED AS AN OSCILLATOR. ASK YOURSELF WHY THE POINT BETWEEN R_A AND R_B IS USED AS THE DISCHARGE, AND NOT V_{OUT} ITSELF.]

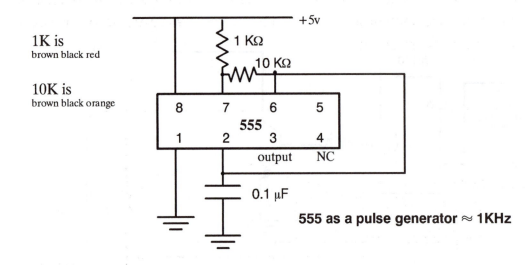

1K is
brown black red

10K is
brown black orange

555 as a pulse generator $\approx$ 1KHz

We show special threshold detector boxes on the RS inputs of the flip flop. We could just let the logic thresholds on the RS flip flop inputs (with an inverter on the R input) do the level detecting, but in the 555 2 threshold detectors called **analog comparator**s are used, for more design flexibility. In a subsequent section, on digital–to–analog converters, we'll see how analog comparators work.

1 .1 .3 Limitations of the 555 oscillator

For Lab 1 and the other labs in this manua,l the 555 is an acceptable oscillator. The 555 can, however, waver slightly in its output frequency. For many engineering designs a "clock" with tighter specs than the 555 is needed. A crystal–controlled oscillator, such as the 74LS124 chip, may be required. The crystal in such a circuit resonants at a particular frequency that can be specified to six decimal places and does not vary due to temperature.

Another WARNING: The 555 is a fine pulse generator, but it is **not** a TTL chip. Sometimes problems with TTL counters in the lab can be traced to a 555 used to drive a counter. The 555 may not have a good enough slew rate (slope) for an edge–triggered counter. PASS THE 555 OUTPUT THROUGH A 7414 SCHMITT TRIGGER INVERTER TO CLEAN IT UP IF YOU SUSPECT THAT YOUR COUNTER (ESP THE '569) IS NOT RECEIVING VALID INPUT...

1 .2 The 654 VCO chip

Recipe for another pulse generator. You will have two chips which can generate pulses—the 555 and the 654. Here is a "recipe" for the 654 VCO, described in more detail in the data sheets. You'll see another version when you do lab 8. This circuit is for a flicker–free, 50% duty–cycle square wave:

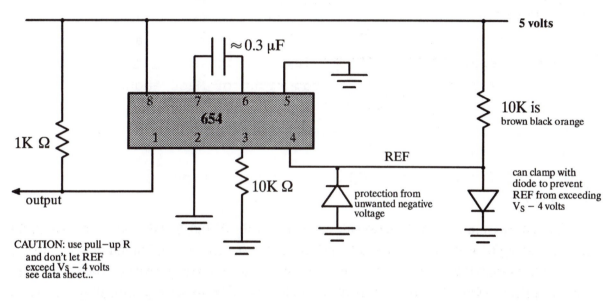

The 654 is more expensive than the 555; about $6 vs $1!

protect the 654 input with a diode!

Lab Two SQ

2SQ   4−bit 2C Squarer

Requirements: Design a combinational circuit which can find the square of any 4-bit 2's complement number. Use MacBreadboard 1.16 layout and simulation software. (That limits the number of chips to one breadboard!) The 4-bit input can come from a DIP switch on MacBreadboard. Be able to display the answer <u>in base 16</u> on the 2-digit hex display on the bottom right of MacBreadboard.

For input of 1000 = −8, the answer will be
$+64_{10} = 100\ 0000 = 40_{16}$
therefore you will need 7 bits of binary output to go to the hex displays.

Discussion: I used the following chips in a design: 7486, 74283, 7400, 7408 & 7410, but you may use what you like from the "Chips" menu of MacBreadboard. Try to be neat in your wiring, and color the wires to be able to keep track of the different data paths. All wires associated with the LSB for example, in my design, were colored **RED**.

You may want to design the solution to everything but the −8 input, then see how you can finesse the input 1000 for the answer 100 0000...

Read about 2's complement representation in Chapter 1 of the text.

INPUT (binary)		OUTPUT (hex)
0−7	−1−8	hex square
0000		0
0001	1111	1
0010	1110	4
0011	1101	9
0100	1100	10
0101	1011	19
0110	1010	24
0111	1001	31
	1000	40

Lab 3−M

3−M Pattern Detection Using Inhibition by Majority Logic

Requirements:

Using <u>only</u> the two CMOS chips MC14506 and MC14530 for logic, build a circuit which responds by lighting an LED when **any two consecutive out of five buttons in a row** on your keyboard or DIP switch are pressed simultaneously. The circuit should NOT respond if three or more buttons or two non-consecutive buttons are pressed.

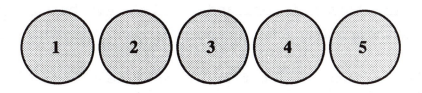

Discussion: Unconnected CMOS inputs may "float" high or low so be sure to force your (un)connected inputs to move towards the values (+5v or GND) you desire. "Pull−up" or "pull−down" resistors may be useful here. 1KΩ may be a good pull−down value. The LED can be driven directly from a chip output.

The Tri−State outputs on the 14506 AND−OR−INVERT chip can be put in high−impedance "disappearance" states by *disabling* them, as shown on the chip's truth table.

Consider what use you can make of the "**E**" input on 14506. Before demonstrating your circuit, make sure that a "1−3−5" input will not light the LED.

For more hints, and an introduction to Neuroengineering, see: JD Daniels, "M−Cells: A logic circuit model to account for some features of CNS inhibition", *Biological Cybernetics 29*: 1−9 (1978).

Note: It is possible to meet the requirements for Lab 3 using MC14506 plus only **one** majority gate on 14530. Think about using an LED from +5 to chip output!

Lab 3–P

3–P   Priority Alarm Test

Use five buttons of your keyboard.

If no button is pressed, the display is blank and an LED is off.

If the button representing ALARM is pressed then the LED lights up, and the display stays blank, even if any three or fewer other sector TEST buttons are pressed.

If the ALARM button and all four test buttons are pressed at once, then the LED goes off and "8" appears on the display.

If the alarm button is off and test button N is pressed, then N appears on the display and the LED is off. <u>N=1,2,3,4.</u>

<u>If the alarm button is off and any TWO test buttons are pressed simultaneously, then the larger of the two button numbers is displayed.</u>

If the alarm button is off and 3 or 4 test buttons are pressed simultaneously, then the display is blank and the LED is off.

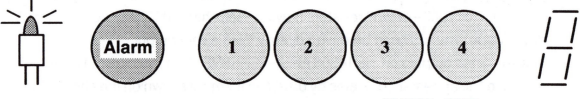

SECTOR TEST

No counter chip allowed in the (hardware) design!

We suggest you try Lab 3P with Beige Bag 3.0.
You should see a 74148 and a seven segment display and a 7447 display driver in the Beige Bag Library.

Discussion:

You can use the DIP switch set instead of the keyboard if you like. Ground one side of the switch and pull up the other side with a 1K or so resistor. Let the output be on the DIP side of the 1K resistor.

A five−input truth table seems to be involved. How many outputs are there?
But maybe you can break the problem up into smaller parts.

Can you use "Lamp Test" on the decoder−driver for the display?
And under what conditions do you need to blank display with "ripple blanking input" on the decoder−driver?
You may need to detect when NO buttons are pressed, when ALL buttons are pressed, and when a majority of buttons are pressed. These detections may be a better input to a truth table than the raw data of the buttons themselves.

3−P is a combinational design; no flip flops or latches are needed. Look at the 74148 data sheet! You may want to use active−low convention for 74148.
And what about the majority logic chip (MC14530) to detect when 3 (majority of 5) or more inputs are active?

Hardware Option: You can borrow a piezo−electric buzzer for the alarm and drive the buzzer with a gated 555 pulse generator.

Lab 4K

4K   Keyboard Encoding

Requirements: Arrange so that each of 16 different buttons on your keyboard represents a different hexadecimal number on one digit of your display. When no button is pressed, the display's decimal point (DP) will be lit, but when (at least) button "F" is pressed, the DP will go off.

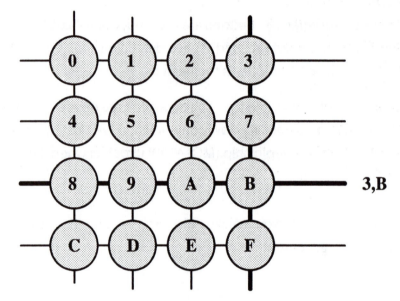

Connecting the row and column wires with a button push

You may have to use the soldering iron in the lab to connect hook-up wire to the "pins" of your keyboard.

Discussion: Consult the 8856/7448 data sheets for the symbols which represent the higher order hex numbers. Note that $F_{16} = 15_{10}$ = blank display so we need to distinguish between F_{16} and no press; this is why the decimal point is used.

Your 20 button keyboard is a matrix of 4 by 5 wires (9 wires total).

When a button is pressed a unique pair of row and column wires is connected (shorted) together. (See figure above.)

Devise a method for determining when two wires are shorted.

(Think of a way to light an LED if two wires are connected.)

You may want to build a circuit which **scans** the keyboard key by key. The scanner will work by sending test signals to the columns while the outputs of the rows are analyzed. For the fault tolerance question we may ask you to predict what response your circuit will give when **two** buttons are pressed simultaneously! Consider how multiplexers and demultiplexers can aid the scanning process.

Suppose a LO output and a HI output are connected together...which one will win? (This can actually happen in *un−buffered* keyboard decoding, when two buttons with the same multiplexer input are pressed at the same time.)

The keypad on a touch−tone telephone: Each of 4 rows and each of 3 columns is associated with a unique frequency tone. When you press a button, for example "3," the resulting sound is the linear sum of two tones, one for the row, one for the column. All of the buttons of a column are associated with the same tone, and all of the buttons of a row are associated with a tone. Can you hear the effect when you press the phone buttons? This set−up means that 7, not 12, tones are needed to encode the 12 buttons of the keypad. It also means that even a person with perfect pitch will have a difficult time whistling into the mouth piece to "dial" a number, since he or she would have to whistle two tones simultaneously. Difficult, but not impossible. Some blind people (who rely on sound more than the sighted) are able to whistle long distance access codes into the phone and call for free their friends in Hawaii.

Lab 4S

4S   Clocked Sequencer with External Control & Halt

Requirements: In the NORMAL mode the circuit will step through the sequence 7, 2, 1, 3, 4, 7, 2, 1, 3, 4, 7, 2, 1, 3, 4, 7 etc. Use a de-bounded button (or switch) which will allow you to single-step through the sequence. The sequence should be displayed. <u>If the display reads 4 and you've switched to ABBREVI-ATED mode</u>, then single-stepping will show 5, 6, 5, 6, 5, 6, etc., otherwise the long

7 2 1 3 etc sequence will display until you get to 4, then the abbreviated 5 6 5 6 will start. If the abbr. display shows 6 and you switch back to the normal mode, then the next digit will be 7; if the display shows 5 (and you've switched back to "normal") then step to 6 before returning to 7.

If you are in the <u>HALT mode</u>, single-step clock will not be able to change the current display. <u>Going into or out of HALT will not change the (correct) display, no matter what the phase of the clock.</u>

YOU ARE URGED TO DO LAB 4S WITH LogicWorks or Beige Bag software on the Macintosh. With LogicWorks layout and simulation software you won't be restricted by the hardware kit's limitation on the number of gates or flip flops available. Read earlier section in Lab Manual about LogicWorks and Beige Bag, and see documentation near lab computers.

Another Lab 4 help from Capalino Computing: Try Karnaugh Works, in the Logic Works folder. No documentation for it, but you can enter the 0's and 1's of your J and K maps then let Karnaugh Works figure out the SOP or POS forms, with or without hazards.

Discussion: Text Chapters 5–7 on sequential logic design relate to aspects of lab 4; particularly Chapter 7. When using flip–flops, be aware that transients in your (hardware) circuit may inadvertently trigger CLEAR or PRESET if those inputs are not pulled to appropriate 0 and 1 values (+5v or GND).

The halt switch, and its relationship to the clock, may be considered a problem in asynchronous logic. You may want to consult supplemental text chapter, "Sequential circuits without clocks," for more advice on how to proceed. Start with a clock–in, halt, and clock–out timing diagram. Otherwise just have <u>halt</u> inhibit all the AND gates leading the the J's and K's, and you turn the halt problem into a combinational solution.

Chart of the sequence. Time going down.

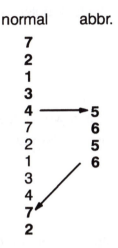

Chart of the sequence with columns "normal" and "abbr." showing the normal sequence 7, 2, 1, 3, 4, 7, 2, 1, 3, 4, 7, 2 with arrows indicating the abbreviated sequence 5, 6, 5, 6.

Note for hardware fans:Flip flops in your kit.

Flip flops are the essence of **sequential logic**, logic with memory, to be contrasted with combinational logic:

Eleven chips in your kit contain flip flops. Three of the chips,

7474 ↑ trig

7476 ⊓ clk

74LS112 ↓ trig

provide separate clock, PRESET and CLEAR lines to each flip flop. These chips may be useful in Lab 4, where you must control J and K inputs to achieve a particular sequencing of outputs. Note that the 7476 clock appears to be the old Master/Slave type...you might want to test the 7476 before using it. Note also that the 7476 is such an old–fashioned chip that power and ground are not at the corner pins...

Exercise: Can you figure out how, using feedback, to turn a D–flip flop, into a JK?

74123 output Q is always LOW unless the correct combination of inputs produces a **pulse**...this is a one–shot and will be discussed in supplemental chapter on asynchronous circuits. You can determine the width of the 123 pulse by a RC product. There are two one–shots per 123. Three of your chips,

74LS174 ↑ trig, 6 bits

74LS373 high level=transparent latch, 8–bits; study data sheets to see where
"transparent" comes from

74195 ↑ trig

have sets of flip flops connected to a *common clock*; such arrangements are called **registers.** The term "latch" is usually reserved for flip flops with level–sensitive clocks, like your '373. Your 4–bit '195 has two modes, a *parallel* load and a *serial* shift.

74164 is a simple 8−bit shift register; all the flip flops are on the same clock (synchronous) but the data for (example) the 8th flip flop must be shifted down 8 clock pulses from the input pin before it appears as output.

The two 4−bit counters

74169   ↑ trig

74LS569 ↑ trig

have their inputs connected internally to generate *synchronous* up or down counts. These chips are discussed in the text, Chapter 7. The 569, a 20−pin chip, has 3−state outputs and an asynchronous clear.

Later you'll receive the

22V10 PAL , which has 10 clocked D flip flops.

Is static RAM—like in your **21C14** or **1423**—composed of flip flops? Read text Chapter 8 on Memory. You also have a dynamic RAM chip, the 514256, in your kit.

Various other chips, such as the 7400 quad NAND and 7402 quad NOR chips can be connected to make unclocked SR latches for switch debouncing.

Lab Five

5   Analysis of Logic Families by Measurement
of Input & Output Voltage & Current

Lab 5 requires you to take measurements on some of your chips. As a consequence you must show a Lab Report to on of the instructors, who will read your report on the spot. If you need to revise any of your answers, that revision can become your FTQ. Otherwise, as an FTQ, we will ask you to repeat one of your measurements in his presence in order to verify some answer in your report. Be prepared to answer your FTQ(s) right away. After signing your scorecard we will save your report until the end of the course, at which time we will "un-save" it. You can do most of the Lab 5 measurements with your (DM27xT) digital multi-meter (DMM).

Try to organize your answer sheet in the spirit of Computer Science documentation standards or Engineering lab report guidelines. PRINT OR TYPE NEATLY! We don't want to waste time decoding your script! We need something complete and legible to evaluate rapidly, while you wait. Read supplemental text chapters on static and dynamic chip characteristics before starting lab 5.

Requirements: Answer the following questions:
Each question to be answered or measurement to be made for your lab report is numbered...for your convenience and organization!

A. Output measurements

Open Collector Outputs: You have three chips with open collector outputs: 7406, 555 and LM311.

(1) With your 7406 powered by +5v, what is the output voltage of an inverter with no pull up resistor and the input grounded (logical '0' input)?

(2) Measure again for the input connected to +5 volts (logical '1').

(3) How does the output voltage for each input state change when a 1KΩ "pull−up" resistor is tied from the output pin to +5v? *Why? Why doesn't a chip like the 7414 need a pull−*

+5 v.

PULL−UP
RESISTOR

up resistor?   [With a pull−up transistor, when inverter input is HI, then the output transistor is ON and the output voltage is called V_{CEsat}.]

(4) What happens to the output voltage when the 7406 pull−up resistor is tied to +12v? DO NOT POWER THE CHIP WITH +12v THROUGH PIN 14! KEEP PIN 14 AT +5v!

(5) What does your <u>data sheet</u> for the 7406 claim is the maximum allowable output voltage?

(6) Speaking of power supply variations, what does your data sheet say a regular 74xx chip can tolerate, as far as deviations from +5 are concerned? There are really two maximum voltages: Above one maximum voltage the chip may burn out permanently; above a lower maximum voltage the chip may not function properly, but could return to correct operation if the voltage is lowered.

(7) What does the 74**C**04 data sheet say about power supply voltage variations for CMOS chips? Some of you may have 74ACT04 chips.

(8) What does the data sheet claim is the maximum allowable **current** that can flow through one output transistor of the **7406** before it BURNS UP? (You could exceed this limit by having a short circuit from +5 supply to **7406** output pin—then if output the transistor is turned on it confronts pull−up = 0Ω and tries to sink too much current.)

(9) How much current flows through the 1KΩ pull up resistor on 7406 when the resistor is tied to +12v and Vout = LOW?

(10) What logic function is realized if five of six 7406 outputs are connected to the **same** 1KΩ pull−up resistor, and the output of that block is connected to another inverter? If you're having trouble figuring this out, hook up the chip and generate the truth table!

(11) Using information from the data sheets about the maximum allowable current for low output, calculate what would be the minimum allowable size of **one resistor** if the resistor were connected between +5v and **all** 6 of the 7406 outputs? The resistor will have to limit current to the output transistors.

[This calculation assumes that the current distributes itself uniformly to all six output transistors, and that all transistors are on; in fact most of the current may head for a path of least resistance through one transistor.]

(12) Imagine two 2−input NAND gates, with open collector outputs tied together and pulled up. What Boolean expression results, if we call the four inputs A, B, C, D? You could try this if we had 7403's or 7401's around.

(13) *Without an output pull up resistor*, is the 7406 able to drive properly a 7414 inverter? Is it able to drive a 74**C**04 inverter? (*Kuribayashi effect*)

3−state outputs: You have five chips with 3−state outputs—MC14506, 74LS240, 21C14, '569 counter and 'LS373.

(14) With your **74LS240** gates **disabled**, what voltages do you measure on an output pin if the inverter input is grounded? (Be sure to power the chip with +5v and GND!)

(15) How does the output voltage change when you **enable** the gate? Draw a <u>logic</u> circuit diagram showing how to configure 74LS240 as a *multiplexer*, like your '158. You can use one extra inverter, and you don't need to put in the '158 <u>enable</u> feature.

(16) What is I_{OHZ} for your 74LS240? How does that compare to I_{IH}? Does that mean a Hi−Z output can "fanout" to one other inverter?

(17) Why are 3−state devices useful for connection to data busses?

B. Input−Output Relationships

Noise Margins.

(18) *Graph*, for the four chips 7414 (~~not LS14~~), 74LS240 (enabled), 74C04, and 555*, *voltage−out as a function of voltage−in* for one inverter each, over the range 0 < V_{in} < 5v. For both the 555 and 7414, graph once for V_{in} increasing, then overlay the data for V_{in} decreasing. Especially for the 555, you should see a good example of **hysteresis**. For the 555, you may need to <u>pull up</u> the output pin 3 or 7 if you use it for output. For the 7414 monitor carefully the <u>input</u> voltage as the chip makes an <u>output</u> transition. If the input makes a sudden jump as you increase it, you may have to make the I/O measurement with a lower impedance input source...like a unity gain voltage follower...see text D to A § (*Homer−89 Effect*). Below we show how to set up the LF353 to act as a unity gain voltage follower.

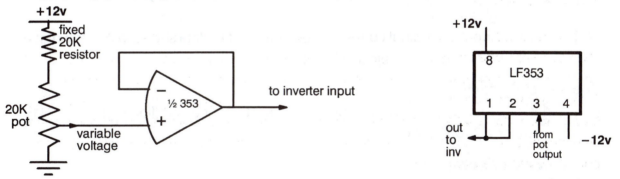

Also shown in the figure, at the left, is an arrangement of resistors which will decreases the mechanical sensitivity of your potentiometer and make it easier to measure the fine changes in output near output transitions. The arrangement will give you input test voltages in the range 0 to 6 volts.

An alternative, faster, method: Use the X−Y feature of an oscilloscope to generate all your curves automatically, with the help of a triangle waveform generator. When you set up the triangle waveform generator, be sure to use **offset**, to insure that the waveform amplitude goes from 0 to +5 volts, and not −5 to +5 volts. The negative voltage may injure your chips. Also, make sure ground of your power supply is connected to ground of the 'scope.

---

* To use the 555 as a plain inverter connect pins 2 and 6 together to be input; use pin 3 for output. and pull it up with 1KΩ. No need for a capacitor to ground on pin 2; this isn't an oscillator!

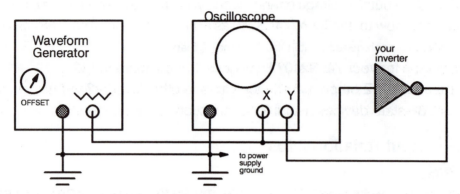

(19) When you're finished drawing the I/O curves, inspect them and calculate the ΔV_H and ΔV_L noise margins for each chip.

(20) Which chip has the best **pair** of noise margins?

(21) Measure the HI and LO thresholds for your logic probe. What is the voltage range for which both lights are off on the logic probe? Use a potentiometer to vary the voltage input to the logic probe.

Fanout

(22) How many **regular** (not LS) TTL gates (on 7414, etc) can one of your 74C04 (CMOS) outputs drive high **and** low?

(23) For typical input and output currents listed in your **7414** data sheet, *calculate* worst–case fanout for a 7414 output projecting to other 7414 inputs.

Unconnected Inputs.

(24) What is the output logic level if an inverter input is unconnected (floating)—for a 7414 inverter, and for a 74C04 (inverter)?

C. Power Consumption

See about current measurement later in Discussion for Lab 5.

(25) Measure supply current and calculate power consumption for your 7414 (try not to use a 74LS14) and 74LS240 chips. Do this current measurement for four cases, as shown in the diagram below. (Connect **all** inputs together high or low—daisy chain.)

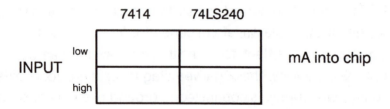

(26) Which condition produces the most power consumption, and why?

(27) How does power consumption change for low inputs on the '14 if one output is

Digital Design Lab Manual

grounded? what if 2 outputs are grounded?

(28) Which kind of **inverter gate** uses less power during <u>open–output</u> conditions?

(29) If the enable of the '240 is "off" does the '240 use more or less power? Note: it's normally not good practice to connect a chip output to ground; we're doing it here just to give the chip output an extreme load. If any current is greater than 200mA (max on the meter) just write "> 200mA current." See precautions at end of Lab 5 concerning measurement in current mode!

Discussion

You may use your **potentiometer** to generate the variable input voltages needed (but see note on previous page, about output impedance). You can make all required measurements with one of the digital multimeters (DMM's) checked out to you.

Noise Margins: Consider a chip which puts out a particular voltage for high or low levels; the input of another chip from the same logic family, connected to the first chip's output pin, will require particular voltage ranges to insure proper recognition of a high or low signal. The difference between what the chip puts out and what it requires as input (for a particular logic level) is the *noise margin*. ΔV_H is the *high level* noise margin; ΔV_L is the *low level* noise margin.

Threshold Voltage: Except for gates with Schmitt trigger inputs like the 7414, there is an input voltage for which the output voltage is halfway between a 'zero' and a 'one' level. This is the threshold voltage V_θ. For curves with hysteresis, like the 7414 and 555, you'll need to calculate noise margins depending on whether the input is rising from 0 of falling from +5v.

Fanout: Assume a chip output is at a high level. The more inputs that one output projects to (fanout) the more current I_{OH} required to *leave* the output pin for various inputs I_{IH}. Addition of too many output loads will cause so much current I to pass through the output resistance that the $V = I \times R$ voltage drop will push the output *below the high level required by the various inputs*. A similar argument with I_{OL} and I_{IL} currents (see data sheets) can be used to calculate a fanout for the *low level* output voltage. The lesser of the two fanout numbers is the "worst case" fanout.

D. Speed and oscillations

Make a ring of <u>five</u> CMOS 74**C**04 inverters oscillate.

(30) What's the oscillation <u>period</u>? frequency?

[You can measure the oscillation period with the "Hz" feature of your multimeter. If you like, an oscilloscope can give you a closer "analog" look at the oscillation waveform of the odd–inverter ring. Two other options: measuring the oscillation frequency on the HP 1651 logic analyzer, or a "counter" in the Tektronix 500–series modules.]

(31) From the period of oscillation, predict the <u>propagation delay</u> of each gate. Does you prediction agree with the 74C04 data sheet?

[Show, by a timing diagram, that the expected period of oscillation of a ring of 3 inverters would be $6 \cdot t_{pd}$, where t_{pd} is the propagation delay through one inverter. Therefore the expected period of oscillation of a 5−inverter ring would be $10 \cdot t_{pd}$.]

(32) What happens if you load one of the outputs of your oscillator with a $0.01\,\mu F$ capacitor to ground? You can measure capacitance with your DMM.

Serial Transmission test: Replace one of the wires in your oscillator ring with ≈ 100 ft of wire (expose the two ends of a roll of wire...).

(33) Now what's the oscillation frequency? Light travels about 1 foot per nano−second, so 100 ft should cause about 100 nanoseconds of delay; you might see much more than 100 ns in your measurement. This is due to the **capacitance** of the coiled 100 ft. Recall the definition of capacitance from Circuits class. Try grabbing the coil with your hand and watching the frequency drop even more.

(34) Which chip is fastest? The basic TTL gate is shown as a NAND. Is NAND the type of TTL gate with the shortest propagation delay? Compare NAND and NOR gates data sheets for propagation delay. Which is faster?

[OPTIONAL: Driving a CMOS with LS oscillations: Attempt to hook up one enabled 74LS240 inverter as an oscillator:

LS240

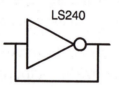

Does your logic probe say the output is oscillating? If not, then hook up a chain of three 'LS240's as an oscillator. *Unfortunately, the maximum frequency response of the LP−1 logic probe is 10 MHz, and the maximum frequency response of the DM27XL is 20 MHz, while the ring−of−three '240 inverters may oscillate above that frequency. You can try a ring− of−seven, or use one of the 60 MHz oscilloscopes to verify the oscillations of the '240 ring.* Now try driving a 74C04 inverter with your 'LS240 oscillator. Does the logic probe or DMM show pulses on the output of the 'C04?

74C04

What's going on? Measure current consumption in the 74C04 while it's being driven by the 'LS240]

(35) not optional!--**Measure the amount of current flowing into a CMOS when it's "doing nothing" and when it's working as a three—inverter ring of oscillators. Don't be surprised if the current flow in a quiescent CMOS chip is too low to measure.** By "doing nothing" we mean all inputs connected high or connected low. What if you let the inputs float!? How is current consumption in a CMOS chip related to frequency of switching?

Multimeter

Most of your Lab 5 measurements can be made in the "**DC**" voltage mode, with a maximum of 20v full scale. Make sure the COMMON terminal of the multimeter is connected to ground. To make a *current* measurement you must switch modes, and probably re—plug one of the meter cables to a "mA" post. Voltage measurements are made in *parallel*, current in *series*. The series connection must be opened up to insert the meter.

DON'T put a meter in current—measuring mode (with probes in current—measuring—mA—jacks) across the power supply or you will blow the meter's fuse! "Across the power supply" means placing the probes directly across +5 and ground, with no resistance in the path! Make sure a chip or a resistor is in between the +5 and ground when you insert the current—measuring leads into the circuit! Even a brief touching of the second probe to ground will blow the fuse! Run a wire from the V_{CC} pin to a safe location away from the chip before making current measurements!

No Joke! Students have blown 4 and 5 fuses in one hour trying to understand the above paragraph! Each miniature fuse costs a dollar!

Remember to take the male probe jack out of the female current receptacle and put it back in the voltage—measuring receptacle immediately after you finish measuring current, so you do not accidentally blow the fuse by trying to measure power supply voltage with the probe in current—measuring slot!

Also: Be careful if you try to change the battery of your meter! Turn off power while you change it! If the battery is (even transiently) put in backwards while the meter is "on," the meter will permanently mal-

function!

Hey! It's happened! A hundred bucks turned to vaporware!

Power: P = V x I. This is true for "DC" circuits,

More generally, for time−varying voltages and currents, instantaneous power is

$$P(t) = V(t) \cdot I(t)$$

The dc−power used within a chip is the product of the current *through* the chip (from its V_{CC} terminal to its GND terminal) times the voltage *across* the chip.

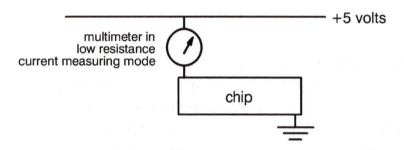

Measure current with the DMM for the 7414 and 74LS240. Put the meter *in series* with the supply and the V_{CC} pin of the chip. Make sure the meter is the **only** path from power supply to chip. *Once a meter probe is placed on the 5v supply, be careful not to touch the other probe of the meter to ground, or you will blow the fuse!* If the meter doesn't register any current, **check the fuse,** or ask the TA to do it. Generally the "20mA" or "200mA" range should be appropriate for chip current measurements.

Parallel and series measurements. A voltage measurement can be made in parallel with other components in the circuit. A current measurement must be made in series, such that there is no other path for current to follow−−all current must go through the meter. See above diagram and not that the power wire normally in place from +5v to the chip had to be pulled out and replaced with the meter. In the current−measuring mode the meter has a low resistance. In the voltage−measuring mode the meter has a high resistance.

Note 1: A situation more dangerous for your inverter chip (than having its output grounded while the input is low) is to connect the output directly to +5v, and set the input high. In the latter case an output transistor is ON and trying to sink a large amount of current; it will heat up (feel it with your finger), if not burn out.

Note 2: It would be informative to measure the current consumption on the CMOS 74C04, but that value is so low (μA) at static conditions that it requires a special amplifier to detect the value using the Wavetek DMM. On the other hand you should be able to measure a significant current through 74C04 if you set up the chip as an odd−numbered−inverter type oscillator, as you will have done earlier, in part D of Lab 5.

Help: Read supplemental chapters on gate—level characteristics, static and dynamic. Remember——the answers for lab 5 don't have to be correct for you to hand it in and have JD read it; if you have missed a question it will just form part of your FTQ.

Plagiarism: We may compare your report with other Lab 5 reports; If it is a word—for—word <u>duplicate</u> of another report, you will be questioned about how your work could be so similar to someone else's.

Otherwise, you're encouraged to collaborate with your fellow students.

Lab Six-C

6-C   Content-addressable Memory

Requirements:

You now have a SRAM chip (~~2114 of size 1K x 4 bits,~~ or 1423 of size 4K x 4 or new SRAM for 1997...), an EPROM (2764 or 27512) of size 8K x 8 bits, and another 4-bit counter. Design an address system which can access 256 locations = 2^8 = 8 bits of address for each memory chip; you need a total of 256 + 256 = 512 = 9 address bits. The 256 EPROM locations you want are actually in addresses $2XX_{16}$, so tie EPROM address pin A_9 high and <u>the other higher order address bits low</u>. Let the output of the memory system be 4 bits; for the EPROM, use the lower four bits of output (O_0 to O_3); you will have to "bus" the two chip outputs together, using their 3-state feature.

On your three digit display show the 8 bits of address and 4 bits of data. For the 9th address bit, have an LED light.

In the EPROM we have programmed some 4 bit codes. For example, at address 200 is word "11". You will be asked to find a few of the ROM locations where the codes are. If your system is successful finding the <u>one</u> location of a pre-programmed code, display its address; if no code is found have a "FAILURE" LED come on. Use 4 bits of a DIP switch to generate the code to be searched for.

<u>Here is an optional "multiple-light specification"</u>: If more than one ROM location has the specified search code, make a "MULTIPLE LOCATION" LED come on; you can display <u>any</u> valid location where the code is.

You must be able to WRITE 4-bit data into any of the 256 RAM locations. The address for writing can be specified on one of your two 8-position DIP switches. On 4 bits of your other DIP switch code the number to be written into RAM.

Your system will have three modes: A WRITE mode for storing values in RAM, a READ mode which will display the current address and contents, and a SEARCH mode for finding which EPROM location contains an asked-for 4-bit code. The search mode will halt into the read mode. The diagram below is a schematic suggestion of an "architecture" for this lab.

Suggestion for the Content–addressable Memory Lab. Your design cloud may need to control the various knobs shown in the circuit. The design cloud may contain other DIP switches that are changed manually.

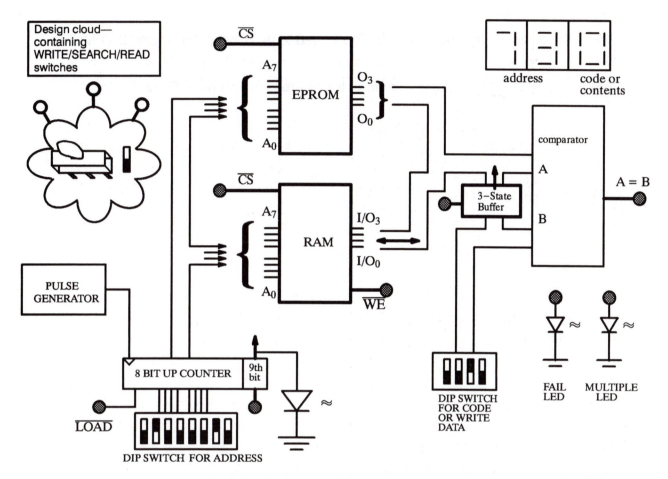

Here's a synchronous way to hook up two 4–bit counters (''169, '569) to form an 8–bit counter: (LOAD = parallel enable—an active low pin—should be tied high to allow counting.) See more about this circuit in chapter 7 of the text.

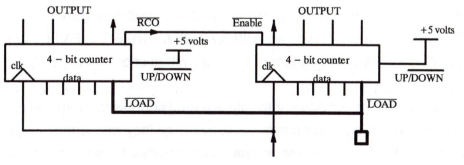

To place a code from your DIP switch onto the address bus, hook up the DIP switch to the data–in pins of the counter, pull LOAD low **and** send in a clock pulse. The chip won't LOAD without a clock pulse.

To drive the three digits of your display, you'll need to use both of your quad 2→1 MUX's.

What's in the EPROM? Here are some of the addresses with non–FF contents:

address	contents, in hex
200 or 280	11
201 or 281	33
202 or 282	44
203	EE
204	66
205	88
206	99
207	AA
208	CC
209	00
20A	AA
20B	EE
20C	DD
20D or 28D	11
20E or 28E	33
20F or 28F	55

THERE ARE NO 2's, 7's or B's.

When we test your Lab 6C: First we will give you a couple codes to **search** ROM for. Your system should deal correctly with the codes (DISPLAY OF ADDRESS, or FAIL). For example, there is no "7" in the 2XX memory page, so your system should FAIL on 7.

Next, we will ask you to write a few values into different RAM addresses, then read back the values verifying that the data numbers stayed in the locations they were originally entered. When verifying, you will be in the READ mode, and you can touch only **address** switches, to set in a new address.

Digital Desgin Lab Manual

We may also ask you to **read** the contents of a ROM location, such as 203_{16}.

If your circuit passes, then you're ready for your FTQ!

Discussion: Read the memory Chapter 8, especially the part on CAM, before attempting this lab. FTQ's for lab 6C may come from problems at the end of Chapter 8. Other possible FTQ's may concern the counters addressing memory during search—what if the count direction is changed on one of them?

Content–addressable memory is used in CPU caches and in neural networks. In *associative* memory only a fragment of the desired code need be presented to the system; the closest match will be found by the associator.

You may receive a 2764 or a 27512 EPROM chip.

There are data sheets for both kinds of EPROM.

IF YOU HAVE A 27512 EPROM, GROUND PINS 1 AND 27 (address pins).

Note that Input and Output of static RAM chips 2114 or 1423 share a common set of wires, so you will need to establish control of the **bus**** during read and write cycles. Pay attention to the read and write cycles shown in the data sheet to insure your WRITE mode works properly. Notice in the figure above use the the 3–state buffer from input A to input B on the comparator. When the 3–state buffer is enabled, writing to RAM will be possible.

When using the 7485 comparator chip don't forget to deal with its cascading inputs!

Next Lab. RAM will be needed for the Time Stamper lab 7, that you may want to attempt immediately after completing lab 6C.

** A bus is a set of parallel wires with a specificed protocol (assignment of meanings) so that devices attached to the bus "know" what to expect of each wire. For example, two of the wires may be assigned to +5 volts and ground for all attached devices. As you can see from this lab, an address bus, a data bus and a control bus are other possibilities.

Lab Six-D

6-D Dynamic RAM Refresh

```
Refresh 2⁸ locations of dynamic RAM chip MCM514256.
Be able to write and read from any of these locations.
Use an 8-position DIP switch for the address to be written to or
read from.
The display need only show the one digit of contents (for the
address set in the DIP switches).
When we test your circuit we will try three different addresses,
to make sure you're not writing the same value to all cells in
the same row or same column. Once the data are written into the
three locations, we will be able to flip between the three ad-
dresses and see the expected different 4-bit words.
```

Read the part of Chapter 8, Memory, which discusses dynamic RAM. Your FTQ may come from questions at the end of Chapter 8. If we slow your clock down by an order of magnitude, will the dynamic RAM fail to remember? Try it!

Read the data sheets for the MCM514256 DRAM chip, including the two-page application note on "DRAM Refresh Modes" at the end of the data sheets.
THE POWER AND GROUND PINS ON THE DRAM ARE THE OPPOSITE OF WHAT YOU HAVE BEEN SEEING ON 7400-TYPE CHIPS!
Note that the data sheets says DRAM must be refreshed every 8 msec.
You may want to use "burst mode" $\overline{RAS}$-only refresh, for which you will need 8 bits of counter external to the MCM514256. The "DQ" pins on the DRAM chip are used for both input and output.
Study the role of $\overline{CAS}$ during the **write cycle**. What if $\overline{WE}$ is LO but no $\overline{CAS}$ pulse occurs? Will a write to address still occur? You may be able to use this to write in a more efficient way...while refresh is going on, the so-called $\overline{RAS}$-only refresh mode.

Tie the higher order address pins to ground.
In the standard "early write" mode $\overline{WE}$ falling edge must occur after $\overline{RAS}$ and before $\overline{CAS}$.

Discussion. Consider the diagram below:

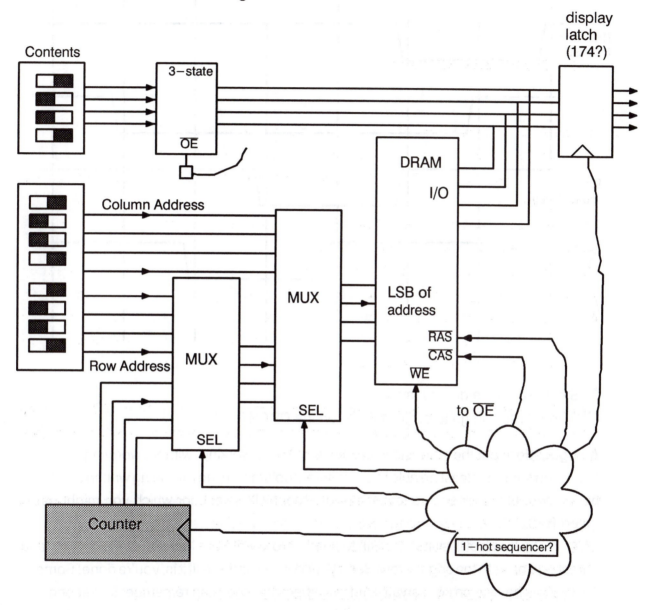

You may want to use a shift register "state machine" in the design cloud.
What should control the $\overline{OE}$ on the data bus, and when?

Here's a timing diagram, lined up with the seven outputs of the 1−hot sequencer.
A 555−through−a−7414 is the clock for the 74164.

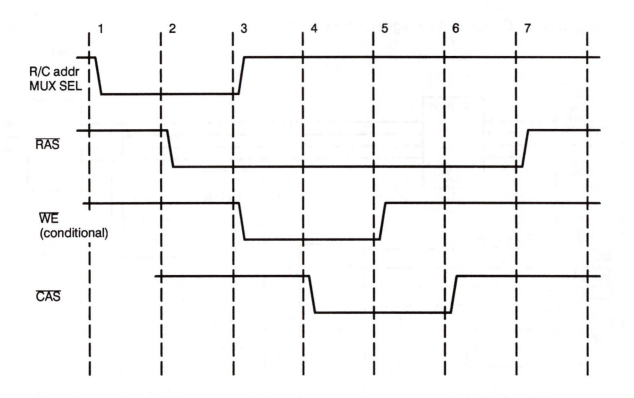

$\overline{\text{CAS}}$ can work as a display latch.

$\overline{\text{RAS}}$ and Write can go to output enable on the DRAM.

A suggestion: get the read and write for a single row working, without worrying about re-fresh. You should at least be able to see different columns in the row being written to. All that needs controlling for such a test is the row−col MUX select, for which you might use a gated RAS.

Then, for the heck of it, switch the DIP to another row. write to a location there. Without any refresh, go back to the original row. See if your data is still there. If it is, you're done! Some of the DRAMs have such conservative refresh specs that they can remember for seconds in-stead of msec's.

For some 514256's you can even turn off the power and turn it back on and the data will still be there!

Lab Seven

7   Time Stamper

After you press the "start" button, your Time Stamper will run
for approximately 16 seconds of "acquisition time". During acquisition time, your display will show the "time" (in hex seconds) and when you press the "event" button your system will
<u>remember</u> the time--up to four events per acquisition interval.
After the acquisition time has elapsed, switch to the "review"
mode; during review your system will display <u>when</u> each of the
four events occurred. You must be able to "single-step" through
the review of events. The accuracy should be ±0.5 second.

Discussion:
Let us say that an **event** is the **start** of a button push--the rising edge. Your system
should discount how long the button is held down. You may need **debouncing** to make
sure that <u>one</u> event button push does not get recorded many times.

Example:

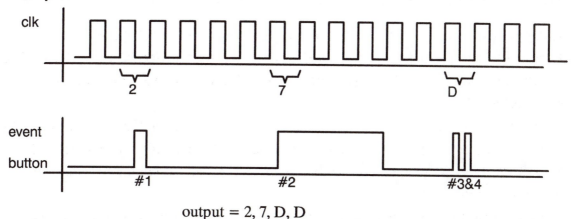

output = 2, 7, D, D

Your display should show the timer output ($0-F_{16}$) during acquisition, and the contents
of RAM during review modes.

Use static RAM for this lab.

Troubleshooting advice: *Don't* make your 2–bit addressing counter a ripple counter or it may pass through unwanted states. Keep the $\overline{\text{WE}}$ (= write–enable active–low) pulse away from the edges of the addressing changes, to avoid other timing problems.

You may want to send the debounced event button into a one shot (74123). Consider what to do with Q and $\overline{\text{Q}}$ outputs in order to avoid timing problems.

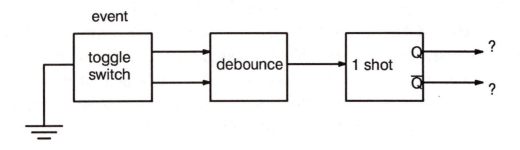

Digital Design Lab Manual

Lab 8

8   Multiplying Digital–to–Analog Converter (DAC) Demonstrating Exponential Decay

Design and build a circuit which sends the output of an 8-bit down-counter into an 8-bit multiplying DAC, and uses the output of the DAC to drive a voltage controlled oscillator (VCO), which in turn closes a loop and provides the pulses for the counter. The reference input for the DAC is adjustable and can come from a potentiometer (0 – 5 volts). Be able to reset the counter to FF_{16}, to start the decay process. <u>Display the two digit output of the counter</u>. If the counter reaches 00, makes sure it doesn't roll over to FF_{16}.

The figure below illustrates what we're talking about.

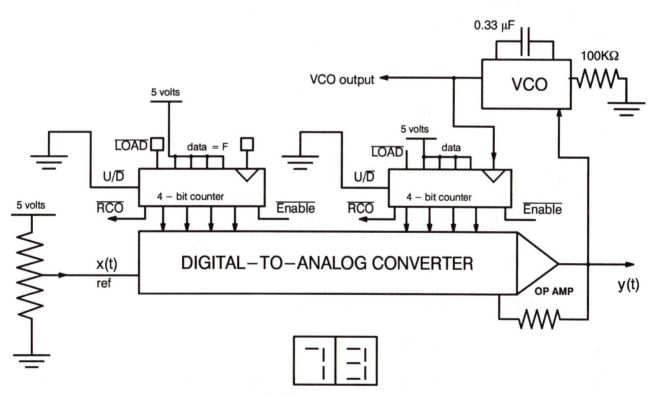

display of counter output

Why does this circuit compute an exponential decay? Recall the definition of the natural logarithm:

$$\int_{1}^{x} \frac{dt}{t} = \ln(x)$$

Think of the down–counter as a negative integrator; but for this derivation we won't put the minus sign in until the end. Call the output of the DAC y(t), as shown on the figure above. The VCO–counter combination integrates y(t) and gives us the following "feedback" equation, where x times the integral of y(t) = y(t)

$$x(t) \cdot \int y(t)dt = y(t)$$

let x(t) be a constant (like it will be, coming out of the potentiometer)

$$K \cdot \int y(t)dt = y(t)$$

take the derivative of both sides

$$K \cdot y(t) = \frac{dy(t)}{dt}$$

rearrange terms

$$K \cdot dt = \frac{dy(t)}{y(t)}$$

integrate again (indefinite form)

$$\int K \cdot dt = \int \frac{dy(t)}{y(t)} = \ln[y(t)]$$

$$K \cdot t = \ln[y(t)]$$

make each side become a power of e

$$e^{K \cdot t} = e^{\ln[y(t)]} = y(t)$$

remember that you're using a DOWN counter, so put in a minus sign:

$$y(t) = e^{-K \cdot t}$$

The rate at which y(t) decays from hex FF will be determined by the size of the input K and by the VCO parameters.

Digital Design Lab Manual

Discussion: Read the supplemental Chapter on D to A conversion before attempting this Lab. And there are additional notes following this write up. In particular, pay attention to how a multiplying DAC is formed. The arrangement of Lab 8 has implications for neural networks. In a neural network, modifiable synapse (connection) sensory input is multiplied by CNS feedback to form a term which governs the rate at which the synapse changes value, either positive or negative. In turn, the sensory input is multiplied by the synaptic weight, and this value is sent to a sensory amplifier.

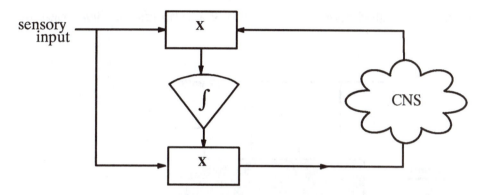

In Lab 8 we've made made a circuit which has the required CNS feedback, but no multiplication by the sensory input. Another engineering term for this arrangement: adaptive gain control, or in the version you implement here, negative feedback. The electronic synapse lab has more information about neural networks.

8–bit counter with no rollover. Your kit (after you finish Lab 5) has two 4–bit counters which can be connected together for an 8–bit counter; you built an 8–bit counter for Lab 6. [Remember, there are two ways to make an 8–bit counter out of two 4–bits: You can cascade the ripple–carry–out of one chip into the clock of the other, or you can make a synchronous counter by connecting both clocks together and sending ripple carry out from the lower order chip to the enable of the other. You've probably done such a counter already, for lab six.]

Preventing rollover: *To make the counter stop at 00 when it's counting down consider what to do with the $\overline{RCO}$s of the two counter chips. When both $\overline{RCO}$s are zero the counters should be disabled.*

VCO. Your DAC chip requires an op amp on its output; see data sheets for the arrangement; the Schottky diodes in the data sheets' schematic are not necessary as long you you ground the chip and op amp properly. Remember to hook up +12 to pin 8 and −12v to pin 4 for power to the op amp. **The VCO chip, AD654, should be set up to receive only positive inputs. Make sure the output op amp from your DAC sends positive, not**

Digital Design Lab Manual

negative, voltages to the 654. If the 654 is set up to receive positive voltage inputs then is given a large negative voltage instead...poof...it becomes vaporware. If your op amp puts out only negative voltage, you can configure your VCO to handle negatives if you like. Consult the 654 data sheet. Check the DAC op amp output voltage with your voltmeter before you connect it to the 654 input. The values for capacitor and resistor shown attached to the 654 in the figure should give you a reasonably slow pulse rate so you can watch (and time) the exponential decay.

We show here suggested connections for the 654 to handle positive voltages:

Notice that pin 8 is connected to +12 volts, while the output is pulled up to +5 volts. The resistor hanging on pin 3 is 105Ω, so that the 654 puts out a reasonably slow pulse rate, which you can watch decay on your display.

Notice in the data sheets that switches in the 7524 ladder choose between OUT2 (ground) and OUT1 (op amp input). The op amp input (negative) will be a virtual ground. You will only be able to see the *voltage* output of the DAC by monitoring the op amp output. If you place a *current measuring* device on OUT1, you'll be able to see an output without the need for an op amp, but using an ammeter is more awkward than using the op amp itself as a current–to–voltage converter.

Possible FTQ's: What happens to DAC output if OUT2 on the 7524 is not grounded? Explain what happens if the up/down control of the counter is taken over by the following circuit:

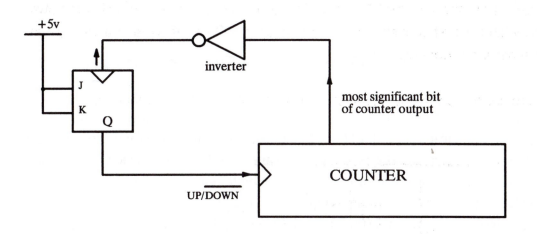

You should be familiar with how to compute gains in op amp circuits, as discussed in the Supplemental Chapter. Related questions to think about:

What happens to analog DAC output if R_{fdbk} is removed from the op amp circuit?

What happens to output if the MSB DAC input is connected directly to a −5v input?

What will happen to the output of your circuit if V+ on your op amp is connected to ground through a 20KΩ resistor?

MULTIPLYING DAC CHARACTERISTICS

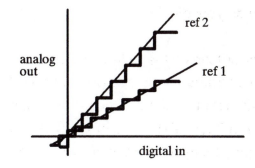

2 Op Amp Tutorial

2 . 1 Practical matters for the 353 op amp and 7524 DAC

You'll need to use an op amp, the LF353 (whose pinout is shown in its data sheets) to generate a DAC output voltage which you can measure with your voltmeter. **The op amp requires ±12 volts for power.** Use your Digital Multimeter for checking voltages.

The Schottky diode shown in the 7523 data sheet's Fig. 1. is not necessary.

To pin 14 (V_{DD}) of the 7523 (or 7524, with latch) you should apply **+5 volts** power; the 7523 is expecting the power supply voltage to be about equal to logical 1 on the digital inputs. If you put +12 volts on pin 14 the 4 or so volts of logic 1 on the digital inputs won't seem large enough to the chip. **You should disregard the "+15v V_{DD}" on pin 14 in the data sheet for 7523.** Notice that the 7523/24 has a feedback resistor for the op amp built in to itself, so you don't need to attach one externally. Simply ground the + input, hook the minus ($-$) input to the *current* output (OUT_1) of the 7523, and feedback the op amp output to the "R_{fdbk}" pin, as shown in the 7523 data sheet.

You may want to generate ±8 volt output for a less than ±5 volt input = V_{REF}. The first op amp on the output of the DAC is an **inverting** amplifier, whose maximum output (at D = 1111 1111) is $-V_{REF}$. You need to boost this basic output by a factor of two. Try passing the first op amp's output through a second op amp (on the same 353 chip) with a gain of -2; this operation will get rid of the inversion at the same time. It's not necessary to do any 2's complement manipulations for the multiplier lab; the 7523 handles positive and negative V_{REF} with no problem. Use your potentiometer in series with a couple of resistors to generate the $\approx$ ±5 volt input:

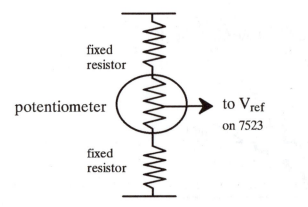

or see the specific suggestions in the Lab 8 write–up.

Another way to multiply with a DAC: hang a 20K resistor from OUT_1 to ground; pass the the resulting signal from OUT_1 to a **non–inverting** op amp with $R_1 = R_2$ for a gain of +2...you can leave OUT_2 and R_{fdbk} unconnected with this approach.

2 . 2 Analysis of op amps

To begin our analysis, imagine a resistor, say $1K\Omega$, hanging in space, not attached to anything. Is there any voltage across it? Can any current flow through it? In general, it depends on the status of the electric and magnetic fields around the resistor voltage, for example,

$V = - \int \mathbf{E} \cdot \mathbf{dl}$; i.e., the resistor may act as an antenna...but for how we want to think about it here, there is no voltage drop, no current flow. Next attach a voltage source (battery) to one end of the resistor, and consider the other side of the battery "ground." We still don't have any current flow because we haven't closed a loop for current to flow around. But at least we know the voltage on **both ends** of the resistor, namely the voltage V_{CC} of the battery.

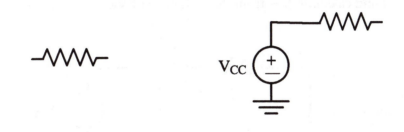

Next attach another battery to the other end of the resistor.

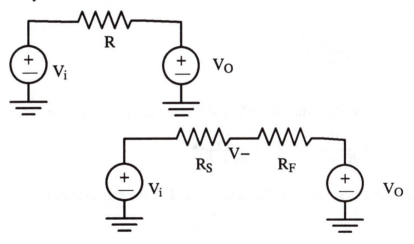

Using Ohm's Law we can compute the current flow through the resistor, because we know the voltage on both of its ends (voltage wrt ground). By the way, if V_i and V_o are different, and R=0, we have big problems...the two voltage sources compete (sparks fly!) to determine the one voltage.

Now add a second resistor, R_f, and call the first R_s. What's the voltage in the middle? (which I'll call V− notation to be explained later). Here's a way to calculate V−, using linearity and superposition. First let V_o be 0, which means it's a **short circuit.** Now calculate V− from the influence of V_i alone. We have a *voltage divider circuit.*

Digital Design Lab Manual

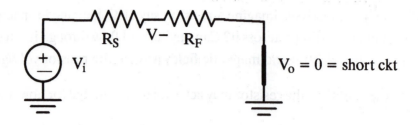

$$V_- = V_i \times \frac{R_f}{R_f + R_s}$$

Next let V_i be 0 and calculate $V-$ from the influence of V_0:

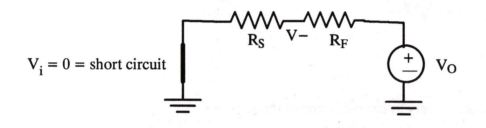

$$V_- = V_o \times \frac{R_s}{R_f + R_s}$$

Now we claim that when both V_i and V_0 are on, $V-$ is just the sum of the two single terms:

$$V_- = V_i \times \frac{R_f}{R_f + R_s} + V_o \times \frac{R_s}{R_f + R_s} \blacklozenge$$

we can do this summation because $V-$ is a **linear** function of its inputs... $V- = \sum_j f(V_j)$

Suppose now we make V_0 a linear function of $V-$, that is a voltage–dependent voltage source. Let $V_0 = -AV-$, where A is a large number. Is $V-$ still linear? And what is its value? [Before we go further, you must know some limitations about Rf, Rs, and A. Let's let Rf and Rs be within a couple orders of magnitude of each other, with R_f bigger than Rs; A will be a big number, 10^6 or so, such that A >> Rf/Rs.] Answer: Yes, $V-$ will still be a linear function, a function $f(V_i)$. And

$$V_- = V_i \times \frac{R_f}{R_f + R_s} + (-AV_-) \times \frac{R_s}{R_f + R_s}$$

Rearranging the above equation,

$$V_- \left[1 + \frac{AR_s}{R_f + R_s} \right] = V_i \left[\frac{R_f}{R_s + R_f} \right]$$

We can ignore the "1" on the left because A is such a big number. Therefore,

$$V_- = V_i \times \frac{R_f}{R_f + R_s} \times \frac{R_f + R_s}{AR_s} = \frac{V_i}{A} \times \frac{R_f}{R_s}$$

We've already set up the condition A >> R_f/R_s so V− must be close to 0...a *virtual ground*.

At this point we're going to re−label everything in terms of **operational amplifiers.** They're called *operational* because they can perform algebraic operations such as summation, on input, as we shall see. We'll make our linear DAC out of one or more op amps, and groups of resistors. Here's our picture of an op amp: See that R_s and R_f are in comparable positions in the op amp circuit as they were in the resistor−battery figure above

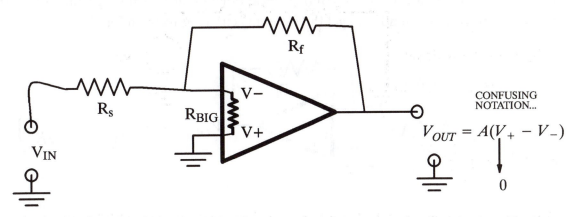

2.2.1 Three properties of operational amplifiers

OP AMPS have three properties which you should remember:

- ✔ Huge differential gain (10^6 at low frequency...)
- ✔ Huge input impedance (10^{12} Ω at low frequency...)
- ✔ Saturating output

Look at the LF353 data sheets, on the second page, under DC Electrical Characteristics:
Input Offset Voltage = 5 mV (typical)
Input bias current = I_B = 50 pico amps
Input Resistance R_{in} = 10^{12} Ω
Large Signal Voltage Gain = 100 V/mV = 10%,
Output Voltage Swing = ±10 volts (for a 12 volt supply).
Maximum output current ± 20 mA
Common−Mode Rejection Ratio (CMRR) = 70 dB (do you remember what a decibel is?)
Therefore, for the inverting configuration shown above, that if the output is not *saturated*

(not at ±12v) then V− must equal −V_{OUT}/Gain = −V_{OUT}/A = nearly zero = virtual ground. The negative input is virtual ground only when V+ is set to 0 v.

The gain A relates output V_{out} to the differential input V+ minus V−; the two inputs V+ & V− are "independent", connected by only a small conductance (high resistance). Almost no current can flow between the V+ & V− terminals. Consider the op amp hooked up with R_f and R_s, as shown, with V+ grounded. Look again at equation ◆ above. If V− = 0 then

$$V_{out} = -V_{in} \cdot \frac{R_f}{R_s}$$

Voila! The basic gain formula for an op amp. (Notice the minus sign.) In fact, if you make R_f and R_s = 10KΩ and 1KΩ respectively, and apply a V_{in} of 1 volt, you will read −10 volts on the output of the op amp; and virtual ground will be virtually zero volts.

What happens to our linear amplifier if we hang another input V_{in2}, through another resistor, $2R_s$, onto the virtual ground? We get the following circuit & formula for V_{out}:

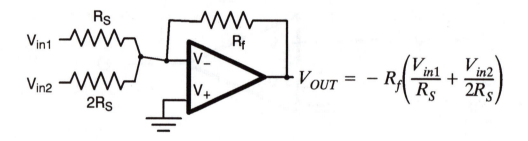

$$V_{OUT} = -R_f\left(\frac{V_{in1}}{R_S} + \frac{V_{in2}}{2R_S}\right)$$

If we let 1 = V_{in} = V_{in2} when they're active, here's the "Truth Table" for this circuit:

Vin	Vin2	Vout
0	0	0 volts
0	1	1/2 R_f/R_s
1	0	R_f/R_s
1	1	3/2 R_f/R_s

This is just what we want for a DAC: Different V_{in}'s representing different significant bits of a digital number. We can add more inputs, and more power−of−two resistors to achieve more **resolution.** Note that all of this happens "instantly", without clock signals.

You have op amps in your Bag−O−Chips, in the form of LF353, two op amps per chip. Remember that the LF353 op amp require ± 12 to 15 volts at pins 8 & 4...not the usual 5v and gnd.

2.2.2 Unity gain voltage follower

What about that pesky minus sign in the gain formula? It means that whatever combination of $+5$ V_{in}'s go through whatever resistors, you'll end up with a negative V_{out}. Consider this op amp configuration (UnityGainVoltageFollower=UGVF):

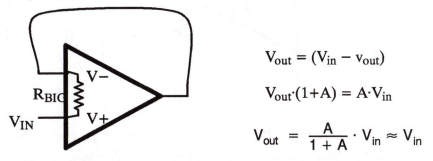

$$V_{out} = (V_{in} - v_{out})$$

$$V_{out}\cdot(1+A) = A\cdot V_{in}$$

$$V_{out} = \frac{A}{1+A} \cdot V_{in} \approx V_{in}$$

This circuit doesn't seem to do much, as far as gain is concerned, but it gets us on the path to variable positive gain. First note that UGVF has another feature, ultra−high input impedance. Consider the current associated with V_{in}.

The current can be computed from Ohm's Law applied to R_{BIG} inside the op amp, between V+ and V−:
$$I_{IN} = \frac{V_+ - V_-}{R_{BIG}}$$

$$I_{IN} = \frac{V_{in} - \frac{A}{1+A}\cdot V_{in}}{R_{BIG}} = V_{in}\left[\frac{\frac{1+A-A}{1+A}}{R_{BIG}}\right] = \frac{V_{in}}{A\cdot R_{BIG}} \quad \text{where } A\cdot R_{BIG} \text{ is the effective } R_{in}.$$

So the input impedance is about $A \times R_{BIG}$. That makes this configuration good for isolation and buffering of high impedance sources, such as piezo−electric devices, phonograph needles, and bio−electrodes.

2.2.3 Output imepedance

The UGVF has a great input impedance, but, in the case of impedance matching, it won't do us much good unless the op amp has a corresponding **low output impedance.** It does. To see this, let's go back and amend our basic op amp model:

Digital Design Lab Manual

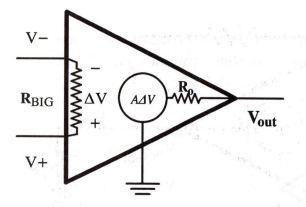

The model op amp features a big input resistance R_{BIG}, a big open−loop gain A, and now an open−loop output resistance, R_o. R_o is in the range $50-100\Omega$.
But the news about output resistance is even better in closed loop forms.

Another digression, about how to measure resistance of circuits with voltage sources in them (such as the output of an op amp). Plot the the V−I curve of a battery+resistor:

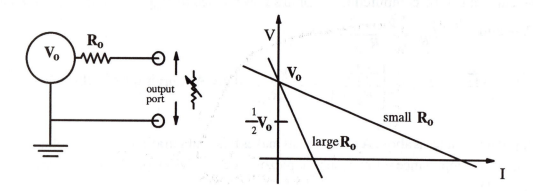

The I−V curves are generated with the aid of a variable resistor at the output port of the circuit. Measure current and voltage at the port as resistance is changed. When variable resistance = R_o, then V = 1/2 V_o.
Graphic version of Ohm's Law: I = V/R.
For a small resistance, a great change in current can result from a small change in voltage. The **slope** of the line is the conductance = 1/resistance. End of digression.

Look at two cases: One is the unity gain voltage follower (UGVF). In our first op amp model an ideal voltage source provides output; the *output* impedance of an ideal voltage source is zero, but in the case of a real op amp, the output current is limited, in a non−linear way (see data sheets for output current curves). For the LF353, 20 mA is about all it can put out. (If you need more, try using a transistor for current gain.) Divide 10 volts by 20mA and we have 500 ohm output impedance. Now consider the following test circuit:

Digital Design Lab Manual

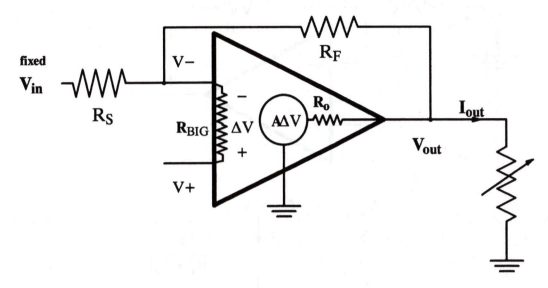

Note first that unless R_O << R_F then V_{out} will not have the desired relationship to V_{in}. Now look at a curve from the LF353 data sheet, Output Voltage vs Source Current

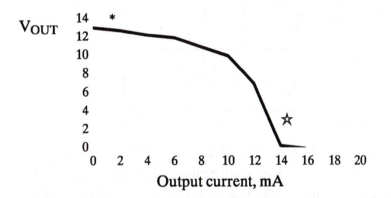

At the point marked * the V/I slope indicates a low resistance; at ☆ the slope is greater and the so is the output resistance. This implies that, <u>at low load current</u>, an op amp has relatively low output impedance. Low output impedance will be useful for testing chip inputs in Lab 5.

Changing UGVF for different gains. Place a voltage divider on the output−to−input connection of UGVF:

Digital Design Lab Manual

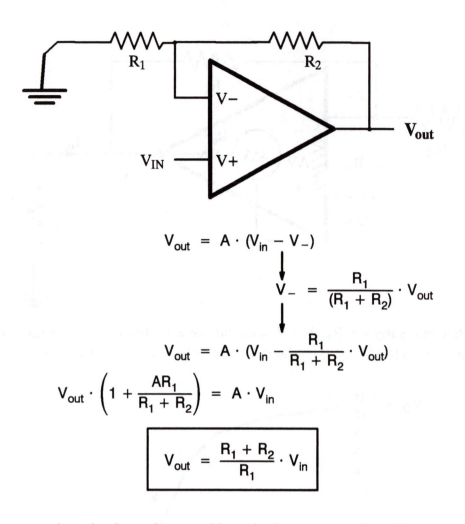

$$V_{out} = A \cdot (V_{in} - V_-)$$

$$\downarrow$$

$$V_- = \frac{R_1}{(R_1 + R_2)} \cdot V_{out}$$

$$\downarrow$$

$$V_{out} = A \cdot (V_{in} - \frac{R_1}{R_1 + R_2} \cdot V_{out})$$

$$V_{out} \cdot \left(1 + \frac{AR_1}{R_1 + R_2}\right) = A \cdot V_{in}$$

$$\boxed{V_{out} = \frac{R_1 + R_2}{R_1} \cdot V_{in}}$$

It's no longer unity gain...it now has a positive gain always greater than 1 (make sure $R_1 > 0$; if $R_1 = 0$ then V− is grounded and V_{OUT} will be huge). However, we don't have the flexibility of being able to add a second input...For that we might as well just invert the minus voltage of an inverting **summation** amplifier, with $R_f = R_s$.

2.2.4 Differential Amplifier

Notice that the op amp configurations we've given you—for negative or positive gain—accept only <u>one</u> input; the other must be grounded. In many cases we have requirements for <u>differential</u> gain...we want to know the voltage between two points on the chest, for an ECG, for example; neither point actually being an official ground. Below is a differential gain op amp circuit which combines positive and negative gain configurations, and gives us a chance to use

superposition in analysis.

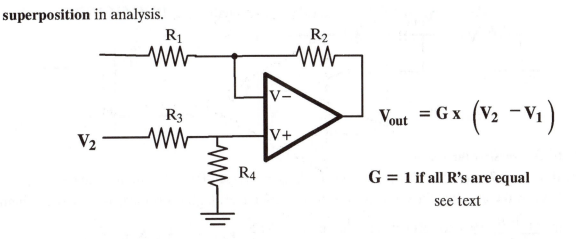

$$V_{out} = G \times \left(V_2 - V_1 \right)$$

G = 1 if all R's are equal

see text

If V_2 is grounded, then we have our circuit from above; no need to worry that there are resistors from V+ to ground...V+ is still at zero volts (of course R_3 & R_4 can't be humongous, or they would tend to disconnect V+ from anything). So with V_2 grounded,

$$V_{OUT} = \frac{-R_2}{R_1} V_1 \quad . \quad \text{If we ground } V_1, \text{ then the input at V+ is } V_+ = \frac{R_4}{R_3 + R_4}(V_2)$$

and we can use the positive gain formula from a previous page:

$$V_+ = \frac{R_4}{R_3 + R_4}(V_2); \; V_{OUT} = V_+ \frac{R_1 + R_2}{R_1} = \frac{R_4}{R_3 + R_4}(V_2)\frac{R_1 + R_2}{R_1}$$

Now by superposition we can add the two V_{out}'s together, to find the *differential* answer:

$$V_{OUT} = \frac{-R_2}{R_1}V_1 + \frac{R_4}{R_3 + R_4}V_2\frac{R_1 + R_2}{R_1}$$

Suppose we make all the resistors equal; then $V_{OUT} = V_2 - V_1$, the differential relationship we want. (What if $R_1 = R_2$ & $R_3 = R_4$?) In practice the inputs V_1 and V_2 may have to be protected by UGVF's so the resistances of the circuit are not affected by output impedances of whatever is being measured (skin, for example, has 100++ KΩ of impedance).

2.2.5 Rectifier

(A unity gain half–wave rectifier passes to output only input greater than zero; if input is less than zero, then output = zero.) Here's another variation of the UGVF worth considering. Suppose we replace R_2 with a regular silicon junction diode. Such a diode begins conducting around 0.7 volts. Now, **if we let V− be the output,** we have the effect of a *perfect* diode, which doesn't have to "wait" until it's less than 0.7 volts to begin rectifying.

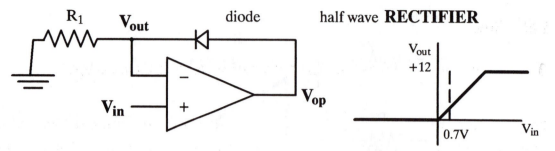

PROOF: consider three cases

1. If $V_{in} > 0.7$ volts then $R_{diode} << R_1$ and $V_{out} = V_{in}$ (see R_1—R_2 gain formula above);

2. If $V_{in} < 0$ volts, then the diode is OFF, has an effectively high resistance, and V_{op} sees a high

gain $\dfrac{R_1 + R_{diode}}{R_1}$ and **saturates** its output at $\approx -12v$; $V_{out} - = V_{op} \times \dfrac{R_1}{R_1 + R_{diode}}$

but since V_{op} saturated at -12, V_{out} will be a small value, because $R_{diode} >> R_1$. In fact, if you set this up on a breadboard, you can measure $V_{out} \approx 0$ volts & $V_{op} \approx -11$ volts. Here's another way to think about this case: Imagine the OFF diode has disconnected V_{out} from any contact with V_{op}, then only R_1 is attached to V_{out} and R_1 is holding V_{out} to ground, or zero volts.

3. If $V_{in} > 0$ but less than 0.7 volts, then V_{op} sees a high gain $\dfrac{R_1 + R_{diode}}{R_1}$ and **increases** until it

turns on the diode at $V_{op} = V_{out} + 0.7$ volts. What is V_{out} when V_{op} reaches its conduction voltage? Return to the basic op amp gain formula:

$$V_{op} = A \cdot (V_{in} - V_{out})$$

$$V_{out} = V_{op} - 0.7$$

$$V_{op}(1 + A) = A\,V_{in} + A\,0.7$$

$$V_{op} = \frac{A}{1 + A}(V_{in} + 0.7) = V_{in} + 0.7$$

$$\boxed{V_{out} = V_{op} - 0.7 = V_{in}}$$

Which is what we want for $V_{in} > 0$.

What if the diode is in the opposite direction? Can we get a half–wave rectifier for negative inputs? Perhaps if two such symmetric circuits feed into a summation amplifier, an absolute value circuit (full wave rectifier) will result. Do we need to invert one of the rectifiers? Will the final output be inverted? Without being clever, you'll use 4 op amps. You'll may need a full–wave rectifier (absolute value ckt) for the Electronic Synapse if you use the 654 VCO chip.

Lab Nine

9 4−bit Successive Approximation A to D Converter.

Design and build a <u>4−bit</u> analog-to-digital converter which uses
the successive approximation method of searching for a 4−bit
digital representation of an analog input signal.

Generate the input signal with your 20KΩ potentiometer (variable
resistor). Continuously show the correct hex answer on one digit
of your display. Your design must be self-starting -- once power
is applied, the circuit must make its conversions automatically,
at a speed able to follow, without perceptible delay, manual
rotation of the potentiometer knob.

To insure that you do not use the "counting" method of A-to-D
conversion, neither counter chip is allowed in your design, and
we may inspect to see that you have not built a counter out of
flip flops. This is not to say that you can't use flip flops...in
fact you have to use flip flops (as latches) in what's called the
SA register.We must see each digit 0 through F appear in proper
sequence, flicker-free, as we rotate the input knob.

Discussion. Read material in the supplemental chapter (and the example worked out
at the end of this write−up) on A−D conversion, before starting this lab. Keep lab 8 (maybe
with different gain... & what should reference for the DAC be?) as your DAC internal to the SA
ADC. You need a "+out" from the internal DAC to match the + signal from the potentiometer. Add a 10−100KΩ resistor between the +5v supply and the potentiometer, if you need
less "gain" on the input.

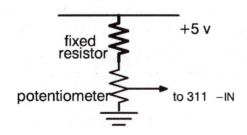

Decide what voltage to power your 311 with. If your 311 inputs stay below 5 volts, then $V_{CC} = 5v$ is fine; if your 311 inputs go above 5v you should hook pin 8 to +12v; pins 1 & 4 should go to ground in either case. No need to connect pins 5&6. Don't forget the output pin 7 is open collector, and may need a pull–up resistor. **Connect the pull–up to +5, not to +12v.**

You can do this lab with clocked flip flops, or with un–clocked S–R latches; <u>using un–clocked latches may be an easier approach</u>. Note that the flip flops in your kit are $\overline{S}$–$\overline{R}$ latches when $\overline{PRE}$ and $\overline{CLEAR}$ control inputs are asserted.

Which four bits of your DAC should you use? Probably the top four, so your signal isn't too small. What should you do with the un–used inputs? Ground them or tie them high? The inputs of the DAC that are involved in the conversion should be driven up to V_{ref}; i.e. if the FF outputs are only 3.7 volts, you may have problems; you may want to have the DAC driven by 5v CMOS outputs (74C04).

Troubleshooting advice: What if you've got the circuit from the SA example all wired up but it doesn't work...and its problem isn't obvious? What to do? Before you do anything else, check with your DMM that, for digital input = 1111, the potentiometer can put out a voltage slightly greater than the largest DAC voltage, and that for 0000 on its digital input the DAC has a nearly zero output. Next check that the comparator inputs from potentiometer and DAC have the + or − polarity you want. Remember that the 311 comparator output is open–collector. If you feel the comparator is "chattering," you can add a 100KΩ resistor from output to the + input; this will put a little hysteresis in the transfer function.

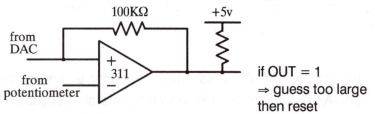

Let's begin systematic troubleshooting: You can go two ways: hook up your outputs to a 1651A logic analyzer, or slow down or stop the clock. Let's assume you've stopped the clock, preferably by pulling the wire off of the 555 or 654 oscillator. (You can inject clock pulses, by touching the loose wire to ground, without de–bouncing, because all you need is to **return** to a particular sequencer state, for a given potentiometer input.) With the logic probe, check that the sequencer has <u>only one high output at a time</u>. Next bypass the output latch and display directly the SA register output. You need to do this because you'll be stepping & stopping through the control sequence, inspecting states before the Q latch signal. Set the potentiometer for a low value which should convert to "0." Now get the first 154 output, Q_A, on the 1–hot–sequencer to be high. Do you see 8 = 1000 on the display? Okay. Next get Q_B to be high. Do you see 0100 = 4 on the display? Good; that means the first FF has properly reset and the

Digital Design Lab Manual

second has been turned on for the next guess. For Q_C on is "2" on the display? You get the idea. At every point where the internal display is wrong, troubleshoot why. After you've got 0 working, try 1111 = F. Both 0 and F should be straightforward to generate because they're extremes of the potentiometer setting. Once you've troubleshot 0 and F, hook the display latch back up, and the oscillator clock. Do the other numbers fall in place? Good, you're done! If not, you can try continuing to troubleshoot with the clock in place, using the logic analyzer and looking for patterns in the mistakes the system makes, or you can go back to the stop & start technique above.

Be wary of using **clocked** flip flops for the SA guessing circuit. In the SA example diagrams, all the FF's outside of the sequencer, and display latch, are plain unclocked SR's. How many sequencer outputs should you use? all 8? That would be the most conservative. Use one Q_N for *reset*, Q_{N+1} for *set* of the next guess...If you need to expand your zero−detecting NOR to 7 inputs, try placing a 2−input OR gate on one of the NOR inputs, or using a transistor as a 7th inverter.

On the *unclocked* SR flip flops you do use, make sure all un−used inputs are tied to something, and not floating around changing state. Yeah, we found out **static** TTL inputs float high, but in a clocked circuit you can't be sure of that.

Trouble with lab 9 is an excellent excuse to hook up signals to the 1651A logic analyzer probes, set the timing and press RUN. Read the logic analyzer instruction sheets for more details.

More troubleshooting: state−skipping caused by one weak DAC output. Suppose your system gives the incorrect sequence 0 1 2 3 5 6 7 9 A B D E F, skipping 4, 8 & C (and maybe F). This could mean the 3rd DAC output is weak and the DAC value for 4 = 100 is actually less than the value for 3 = 011. This is tough to troubleshoot with the logic analyzer, but the pattern of mistakes should tell you what's wrong. Either use a different set of 4−out−of−8 DAC outputs, or get a new DAC. Skipped states are not strictly theoretical. At least one of the DAC's in the chip drawer has a weak 3rd output.

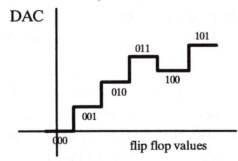

Possible FTQ's: What will happen if the inputs to the comparator are reversed?
What if one of the sequencer wires is pulled out and tied low?

Digital Design Lab Manual

3 Successive Approximation Design Example

In a 4-bit SA conversion, SOC always activates the same first guess: $1\,0\,0\,0 = 8_{10}$. This guess is halfway in the range of possible answers the system can consider:

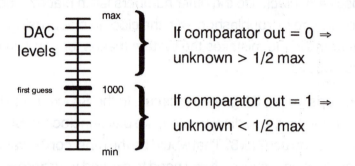

If comparator out = 0 $\Rightarrow$

unknown > 1/2 max

If comparator out = 1 $\Rightarrow$

unknown < 1/2 max

$1\,0\,0\,0$ goes to the DAC, which converts it to an analog voltage to be **compared** with the unknown analog input. If the converted $1\,0\,0\,0$ guess is greater than the unknown, then the comparator will put out a "1". This comparator output goes back into the guesser circuit and inside the following rule is used:

> If guess is too low (comp = 0)
>   then leave the MSB set to 1
>
> If guess is too high (comp = 1)
>   then reset the MSB back to 0

With the MSB decided, the sequence of successive approximations is started and the next guess focuses on the 2nd MSB. The second MSB is set to 1 and a new DAC output is compared with the unknown analog in. The rule stated in the box above is now applied to the 2nd MSB.

As an example, imagine that max = 8v, min = 0 v & the unknown = 5.75 v. The first guess ($1\,0\,0\,0$) results in a DAC output of 4.0 volts and a comparator value of 0. The MSB stays set at 1. The next guess is $1\,1\,0\,0$, with a DAC output of 6.0 volts. The comparator value is 1, so the second bit is reset and the third guess becomes $1\,0\,1\,0$. This third guess results in DAC_{out} of 5 volts, comparator out of 0 v. and no reset of the third bit. After a fourth cycle of narrowing down the range, a final answer of $1\,0\,1\,0$ is achieved.

A "20 questions" yes-no process continues down from the MSB to the LSB at which point conversion is complete. Note that an 8-bit conversion should take only 8 cycles, instead of the maximum 256 cycles in a plain ol' counting converter. What happens at the end of conversion? The guessing circuit knows it has reached the LSB and sends out an EOC pulse, so the answer can be latched for display or placed in memory.

3 . 1 Inside the guessing circuit

Let's look at what must be inside the guessing circuit.

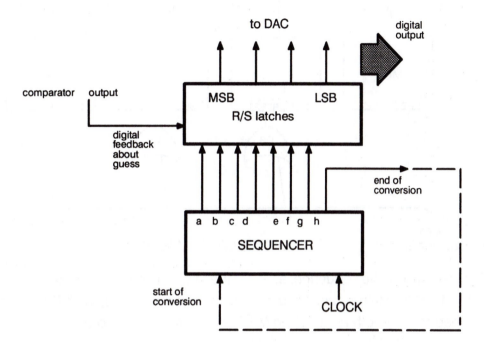

The guesser can be divided into a set of latches (the SA register) and a sequencer. We will consider the sequencer in detail later; for now assume its outputs a–h are high (active) one at time, in sequence (a shift register is involved...). For continuous converting we have shown the EOC output connected to the SOC input.

The SA register is a group of Set–Reset latches:

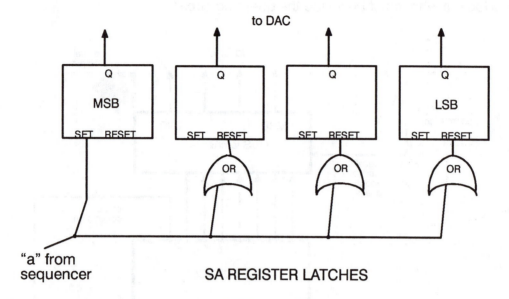

SA REGISTER LATCHES

The first pulse in the sequence, **a,** SET's the MSB and resets the other bits, to establish the guess 1 0 0 0. The next control pulse from the sequencer, **b,** is AND'ed with the comparator feedback: If both are true the MSB latch is reset back to 0.

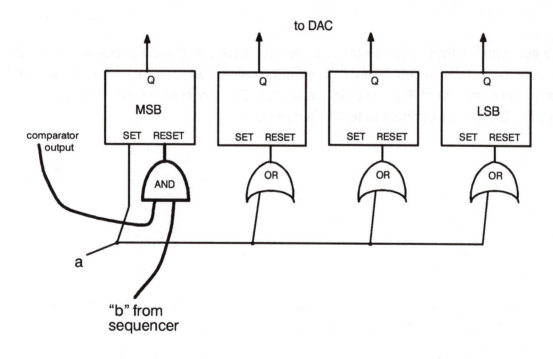

The 3rd control pulse, **c,** SET's the 2nd MSB latch to provide the next guess.

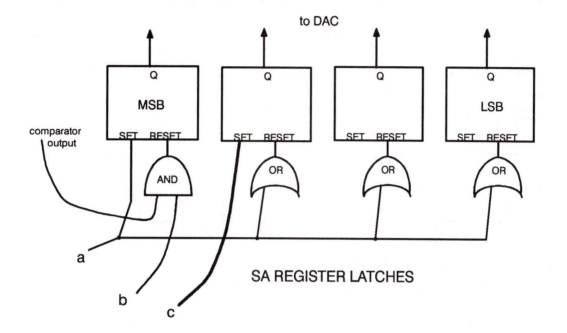

SA REGISTER LATCHES

And, like before, if the comparator returns a value of 1, the 2nd latch is reset (because the guess was too high).

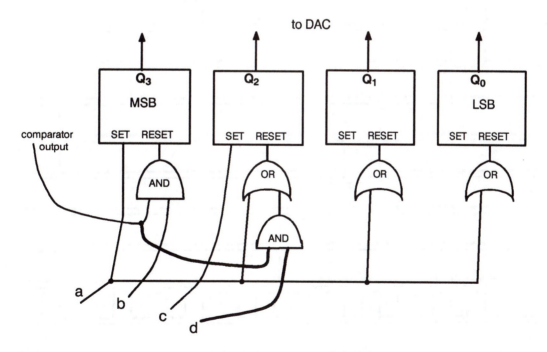

Consider whether it would be possible for **one pulse** to do the work of pulses b & c, that is, have the reset of MSB latch occur at the "same time" as the set for the 2nd MSB.

Observe that there is a gate's worth of delay to reset, and no delay to set, so set may occur **before** reset, resulting in a "timing error," or improper DAC–guess being generated.

The SETing and possible RESETing of latches continues on down the line until the last bit is decided. Note that on the last cycle the *complement* of the comparator itself has the value required for the LSB:

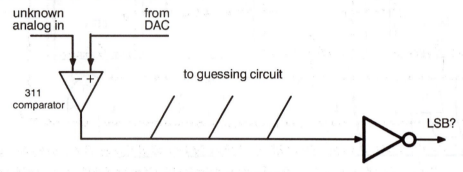

Can you get away with no latch for the LSB?

Probably not...at some point the LSB must be *set* as part of the last guess...

3 . 1 . 1 The sequencer

Let's see what the *timing diagram* looks like for the sequencer output; you can see these waveforms on the logic analyzer if you like:

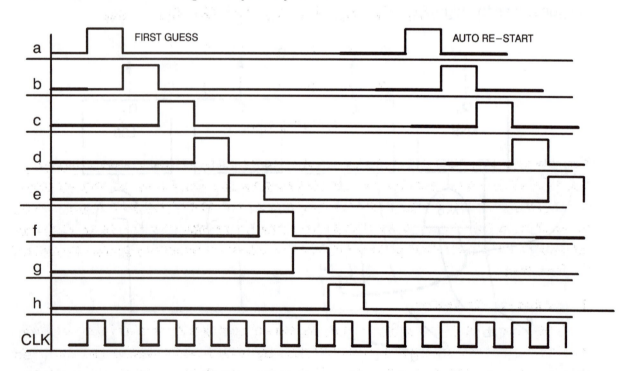

These are the waveforms of a serial shift register, shifting a solitary "1" to the right, then cycling the "1" back to the start:

Digital Design Lab Manual

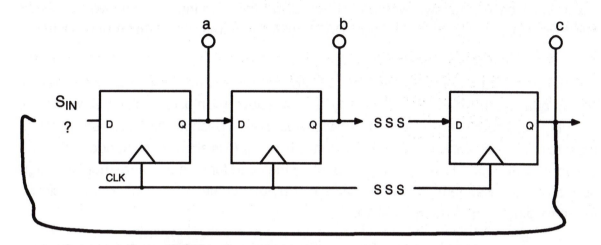

The 74164 serial in–parallel out shift register can do the job of shifting, but if you simply hook up the last flip flop output Q with S_{IN}, you'll have problems: How do you get it to start up properly? What if it drops a bit, or if the sequence picks an extra 1...how can mistakes be corrected?

Consider the circumstances under which you want a 1 returned to S_{in}—there are only two cases (if we're dealing with all 8 sequencer outputs):

	Q_A	Q_B	Q_C	Q_D	Q_E	Q_F	Q_G	Q_H	S_{IN}
(1)	0	0	0	0	0	0	0	1	1
(2)	0	0	0	0	0	0	0	0	1
(3)				anything else					0

The all–zero condition corrects for bit–dropping or start–up problems. Ironically enough, this truth table shows that Q_H, the last stage output, is a *don't care.* All that matters is whether the other bits are zero. What logic operation returns a 1 for all zero inputs, and a 0 for anything else? Once you insert such a function on the input S_{IN}, and hook up the sequencer outputs to the SA register set, you're (essentially) done with the challenging part of the SA design.

3 . 1 . 2 End–of–Conversion

The end–of–the–line pulse from the sequencer can latch the answer from the SA register into a set of latches which lead to the display. By this means the display will be updated only when a *new answer* occurs; other states of the SA register = guessing circuit will be ignored by the display. When troubleshooting you may want to bypass the latch and show directly the SA register state. Notice that SA will always find an answer, even if A_{IN} > DAC-

MAX; in which case the answer will be 1111. Recall that the counting converter would make a mistake for A$_{IN}$ > DAC$_{MAX}$, because the DAC couldn't generate a value large enough to trip a comparator.

Need for constant value during conversion. Look what would happen if the unknown analog input decreased from, say, a value above 1/2max to a value below 1/2max **after** the MSB had been set: A wrong answer would result because all the subsequent bits reset to 0. Then again, what is being converted if the A$_{IN}$(t) is allowed to change during the conversion process? Here we're just repeating the need for sample−and−hold in a high speed converter system. In the SA example, the potentiometer knob is turned so slowly that changing input is not a problem.

```
Consider a CHIP LIKE THE 74LS502, "8-BIT SUCCESSIVE APPROXIMATION REGISTER".
DRAW OUT HOW A CLOCK + 'LS502 + DAC + ANALOG COMPARATOR
It CAN BE A COMPLETE a/d CONVERTER.
```

3 . 2 Converting negative voltages to 2's complement digital form

Assume analog input can be in the range ±V. First let's modify our DAC so it puts out voltages in the range −V to +V:

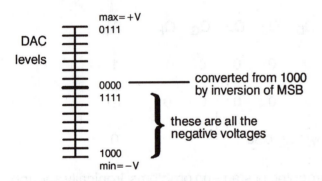

In addition to this adjustment, we need to *invert the MSB* answer bit. Notice that this scheme looks different from the invert−&−add−1 algorithm usually seen with 2's complement. See diagram below—

Digital Design Lab Manual

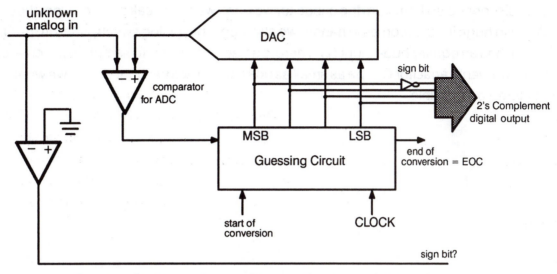

unknown analog in

DAC

comparator for ADC

sign bit

2's Complement digital output

MSB   LSB

Guessing Circuit

end of conversion = EOC

start of conversion

CLOCK

sign bit?

Question: Could we get away with generating the sign bit through a comparator, and eliminate a latch?

```
NOTES...Consider  DAC by R-2R alone...use AD7523, in kit!
```

3 . 3 Sample & hold and analog switches

Consider what a sample–and–hold and analog switch might look like and do. A sample and hold can be designed as:

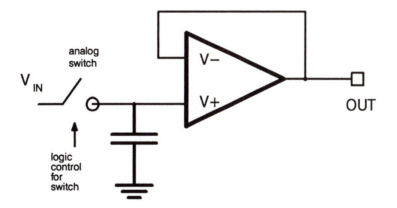

analog switch

V$_{IN}$

V–

V+

OUT

logic control for switch

When the switch is closed (sample) the circuit functions as a UGVF; the high input impedance of the UGVF insures that the capacitor doesn't filter too many high frequencies.

   MORE: "Hold" means remember, remember an **analog** number, for, say, less than a second. Our only analog memory element is a capacitor, so let's charge a capacitor with V$_{in}$(t) and hope it holds...

We'll use our mysterious friend the analog switch to go from sample to hold mode. When

$V_{in}(t)$ is disconnected from from the capacitor we don't want it to leak off its charge; thus the UGVF with huge input Ω comes in handy (we also hope the analog switch, when in the OFF position, has an equally huge input Ω). There is a trade−off here. To sample rapid changes in $A_{in}(t)$, we want capacitor C to be as small as possible; to hold without *droop,* we want C to be as large as possible.

Lab A

A   Serial Transmission & Errror Correction

Requirements: In one part of your system (the sender) place a DIP switch on which you set an 8 bit number from the table of 16 hex numbers shown on the next page. These are the valid 8,4 Hamming codes for a 4−bit message.
In the second part of your system place the display, on which the received 8−bit number will appear. Also on the receiving side have **3** LED's which determine the *position* of a 1−bit error.
(If you know the *position* of a 1−bit error, you can correct it.)
The 8th bit of the code is an overall parity bit, useful for *detecting* 2−bit errors, but we won't worry about the 8th bit here, other than to display it as the LSB.
The separate sides of your system can be connected by only **two wires**, excluding the power and ground wires. In one side of your system there will be a **transmit** button and after you press the button **once** the current 8−bit number will be automatically transferred to the display.
```
Repeat: after the 8 data bits are set in the DIP switch, only one
button (or toggle) push allowed.
```
Please arrange the geometry of your circuit layout so that the two wires can be clearly seen going between separate sub−systems.
You are allowed only **one 74195 & one 7486** in the system. You can dig up four more XOR's in your 74LS382 ALU chip.

Testing your Lab A. First we will ask you to transmit a couple pairs of numbers from the list below... pairs that represent correct transmission without error. Then we will change **one** bit in the message number and ask for re−transmission. Your system should light LED's which tell you **where** the error occurred in the message.
We won't change bits in the Check & Parity code.

Discussion: Read text Chapter 9 on Digital Communication & Serial Transmission. Study how asynchronous transmission can be carried out. See the RS232 example in the text.

If you do Lab A with one wire instead of two, you won't be asked an FTQ. For a one wire solution, the receiver side must have a clock which is close in frequency to the sender's clock. Furthermore, the receiver clock must be started up in phase with the data message, so jitter doesn't cause too much drift in sampling position. Use the frequency−measuring feature of the DM27 or EXTECH voltmeter to calibrate the two oscillators.

Perhaps on the sending side could be a circuit which counts out exactly 10 clock pulses for transmission, and leaves the DATA line HI when a message isn't being sent. Some kind of Parallel–to–serial chip will be needed on the sender side.

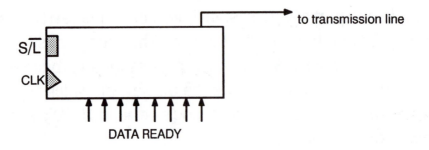

Two modes are required: **Loading** the eight bits on one clock pulse, then **transmitting** the bits one at a time, in the shift mode.
The 74195 is a 4–bit chip. Can you to expand it to 8 bits with a MUX chip (158)?

If transmission always starts with a HI→LO transition, then the receiver will know when to "reset" its oscillator. Find out which pin(s) on your oscillator chips can "restart" the oscillations. Should the transmission end with a STOP bit? How will your receiver know when to clock the SIPO 74164 chip?

Read the part in Chapter 9 about 1–bit error detection & correction. See also the 4–page article by Hamming (parts 3 & 4) which is included after Chpt 9, to find out more about Hamming codes (= linear codes, group codes). You may want to write out the individual 0's & 1's to understand better how the check bits depend on the message bits, and how the parity bit depends on the message + check bits.

In Lab A, you the student do the encoding of check and parity, by referring to the table of 16 allowed 8–bit codes. Normally a circuit would automatically add the extra bits to the message.

Diagram with clouds:

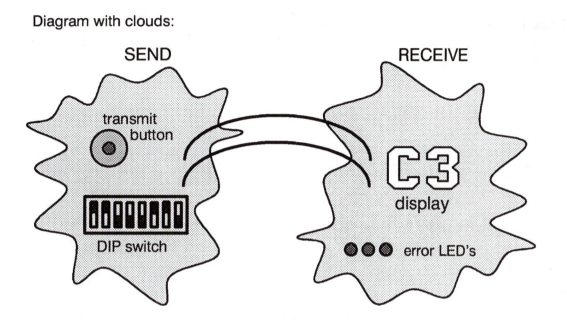

Suggested circuit for the 654, by which frequency can be adjusted through the VCO input on pin 4: Make R and C about equal to the RC combination on the 555 if the 654 is being matched to the 555 frequency.

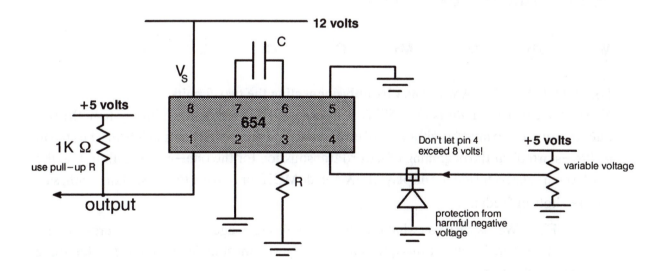

Timing hack: Sometimes a circuit which is losing the LSB on the receiving side can be fixed by putting a properly timed 1–shot between transmitted clock and clock for 164. It may be your last clock pulse gets terminated too quickly. Hey, it's worked on a few malfunctioning Lab A's!

Digital Design Lab Manual

message, check in HEX

0	0
1	7
2	B
3	C
4	D
5	A
6	6
7	1
8	E
9	9
A	5
B	2
C	3
D	4
E	8
F	F

Above are the 16 allowed messages.

M_3	M_2	M_1	M_0	C_2	C_1	C_0	P

For NO FTQ, do Lab A with **one wire only** connecting the two circuits.

You do have **two oscillators chips,** 555 & 654—one will be in each side of the system; the frequencies of the two must be within 5% of each other, and the receiver oscillator must be able to be "re−started" at the beginning of a word transmission for the one−wire solution. Use the clock on the receiver side for display MUX and deMUX, or make a third oscillator with, say, two 1−shots in feedback.

Possible FTQ: We may ask you what the *intended* 4−bit message was if we send across a code with a 1−bit error. To answer this question correctly, you must understand the 8,4 Hamming error−correcting code.

Digital Design Lab Manual

Lab B

B   4 Bit X 4 Bit Positive Hexidecimal Multiplier

Requirements: Build a circuit which multiplies together two 4-bit numbers and displays the eight-bit result. Consider the two inputs as positive hexidecimal numbers--not 2's complement! Enter one of your inputs with your DIP switch, and the other with your keyboard (or another DIP). The keyboard entry may be done by several button pushes, or by one decoded stroke, as you did in the keyboard scanning lab earlier. Your circuit will need a clock. Make provision to single-step the clock--for debugging, demonstration and FTQ purposes. Show that your system accomplishes its result in less than a dozen clock cycles.
Only one 74195 allowed in the design!

If you own an HP 16C or other hex calculator you can check your answers with its hex arithmetic feature. Otherwise the accompanying hex multiplication table shows the 8-bit results we will expect from your circuit.

Discussion: Consider an add-and-shift method for your design. Synchronous and 2-phase clock designs are described in the **Arithmetic Hardware, Chapter 10,** of the text. You should use the 'LS382 instead of the '181 ALU chip. Think about doing Lab B with LogicWorks or Beige Bag. You'll have to create various subcircuits, and combine them into a final design, but you won't be limited by chip selection or timing problems in your Bag-O-Chips.

IF YOU USE LOGICWORKS OR BEIGE BAG, YOU ARE LIMITED TO A TOTAL OF 12 BITS OF ADDERS. THIS LIMITATION MAY RULE OUT A TOTAL COMBINATORIAL DESIGN FOR LAB B. 100% COMBINATORIAL WALLACE TREE and ARRAY DESIGNS FOR LAB B are no longer allowed. SORRY.
Also not allowed: TABLE-LOOKUP ROM solutions IN BEIGE BAG simulations. NO ROM ALLOWED in your design.

Possible FTQ's: What will be on the display if you clock through a 5th cycle?
What will happen if one of the S0 - S3 pins on the ALU is flipped?

Crooked 4 x 4 hex multiplication table:

```
0
1  2  3  4   5  6  7  8  9  A  B  C  D  E  F
2  4
3  6  9
4  8  C  10
5  A  F  14 19
6  C  12 18 1E 24
7  E  15 1C 23 2A 31
8  10 18 20 28 30  38 40
9  12 1B 24 2D 36 3F 48 51
A  14 1E 28 32 3C 46 50 5A 64
B  16 21 2C 37 42 4D 58 63 6E 79
C  18 24 30 3C 48 54 60 6C 78 84  90
D  1A 27 34 41 4E 5B 68 75 828F 9C A9
E  1C 2A 38 46 54 62 70 7E8C 9A A8 B6 C4
F  1E 2D 3C 4B 5A 69 78 87 96 A5 B4 C3 D2 E1

1  2  3  4   5  6  7  8  9  A  B  C  D  E  F
```

In chapter 10 of *Digital Design from Zero to One* study the example of the totally synchronous multiplier. See if you can do something like that design for this problem.

Lab C0

C0   Control of nested subroutines

Here you will build in hardware the guts of a controller for jumping and returning from nested subroutines.

Requirements: First, arrange that three instruction bits, S_0 FE PUP, and 4 DATA bits from a DIP switch are "written" into an instruction register on the falling edge of a clock sent from a debounced toggle switch. There are three instructions, shown below:

	S_0	FE	PUP
CONTinue	X	1	X
JSR = jump to subroutine	1	0	1
RTS = return from subroutine	0	0	0

The instructions will be executed after the rising edge of the clock. When FE is 1 the instruction is a CONTINUE and no registers in Lab C0 change. When FE is 0 then JSR or RTS is in effect. If PUP and S are 1 when FE is 0, then the instruction is a JSR.

A JSR will write a return address (4-bits of DATA) to a memory (RAM) and to the return register, then it will increment a counter that provides the memory's address. [In Lab C* a different address will be put on the stack, but here in Lab C0 the same number will go to both RR and stack.] A RTS will decrement the counter, then clock the memory output into a RETURN register. See Figure on next page.

Notice that you need to display the counter output and the return register contents. Use your hex output chip for one of the displays. You also need an EMPTY LED indicator that detects if more RTS's have been asked for than JSR's previously done.

In fact, such instructions are in the ROM used for Lab C*, but here in Lab C0 the instructions will originate from a DIP switch.

As you can see from the figure below, the instructions need to control several signals: WE of the RAM, enable and count direction on the counter, the RR clock, and the 3-state enable on the

RAM I/O bus. Instruction signals FE and PUP may be able to go directly to the counter.

Design and build Lab C0 with hardware in your kit--no simulation by LogicWorks! No clock chips or oscillators are allowed in your design! When the toggle is quiet, so is your circuit!

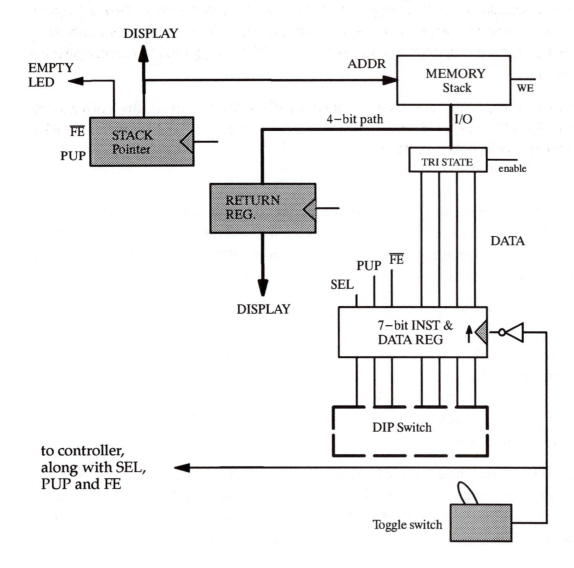

Lab C0 must be completed before you try Lab C* ! (Lab C0 is the design for a critical part of Lab C*, so if you do Lab C* from scratch, you will receive automatic credit for Lab C0.)

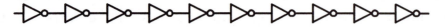

To test your C0 we will execute a series of JSR's, then we will read back the return addresses from DATA by doing an equal number of RTS's. We will do an extra RTS to watch the EMPTY light come on. At various times we will inject a CONT instruction, and the displays won't change.

Discussion:

The principle challenge of the design lies in the timing required to achieve the stack operations. You will need to draw out timing diagrams. During JSR the RR register should be clocked <u>before</u> the stack pointer (counter); during RTS the RR should be clocked <u>after</u> the stack pointer.

Think about a "clockless" controller for these timing problems. Can you think of a way using SET–RESET latches? What about two S–R "delay" lines, one for JSR and one for RTS, with different taps for RR and SP?

Lab C*

"What does not kill us makes us stronger." Nietzsche

C*   Emulation of a Microprogramming Sequencer

Requirements: First do Lab C0!
Construct a circuit which emulates instructions of an Am2911 sequencer. You must handle these five instructions:

	S_1	S_0	FE	PUP
CONT= continue by increment	0	0	1	1
JUMP to D bus address	1	1	1	0
JSR = jump to subroutine	1	1	0	1
RTS = return from subroutine	1	0	0	0
JPP = jump & pop	1	1	0	0

that are announced on four output pins of your ROM, the other 4 being the DATA bits representing a jump address. A series of instructions are in region 03XX of ROM.

$S_1 S_0$ select inputs on a 3→1 multiplexer; for example, $S_1 S_0$ = 11 selects the DATA bits.

PUP is a push/pop signal and controls whether a stack counter goes up or down;

$\overline{FE}$ = file-enable-nought is active-low only when a memory stack is involved, in subroutine (or JPP) operations.

(Note: you do not need to implement the 3-STATE outputs, AR register, or ZERO input of the real 2911 chip.)

Besides 4 bits of instruction plus 4 bits of data, the 2911 needs a clock pulse on each cycle. Your clock pulse will come from a de-bounced toggle switch, and go directly to a 5-bit counter to address EPROM (and maybe elsewhere).

The last page of this write-up shows the sequence you are required to step through ("Expected Y-bus"), and the address in ROM where each instruction is located.

The pin assignment protocol in ROM is

2911 inst	D_3	D_2	D_1	D_0	S_1	S_0	$\overline{FE}$	PUP
ROM ouput pins	D_7	D_6	D_5	D_4	D_3	D_2	D_1	D_0

NO PULSE GENERATORS ARE ALLOWED IN YOUR CIRCUIT. NO 555, NO 654.
If we put a logic probe down anywhere in your circuit (while it's

```
sitting at an address) we won't see pulses. You can have an HP
7340 hex display chip to show your output, if you like. No need
to display EPROM address.
```

In your EPROM, the lab C code is in address region **03XX**. Tie higher order address pins A_9 and A_8 high, and the rest of the higher order address pins low.

We will test your circuit by watching the hex display show the `Expected Y-bus` output from the table while you single–step through the ROM addresses.

Note that for two of the steps you will need to be able to light an auxiliary LED (maybe by having a signal come off of your incrementer circuit) **to indicate a "1" in the next digit.**

Discussion: Below is a schematic that will look familiar to readers of the supplemental text chapter on microprogramming, and the case study that follows, here in the Lab Manual. Also see Chapter 11 of the DDZO text.

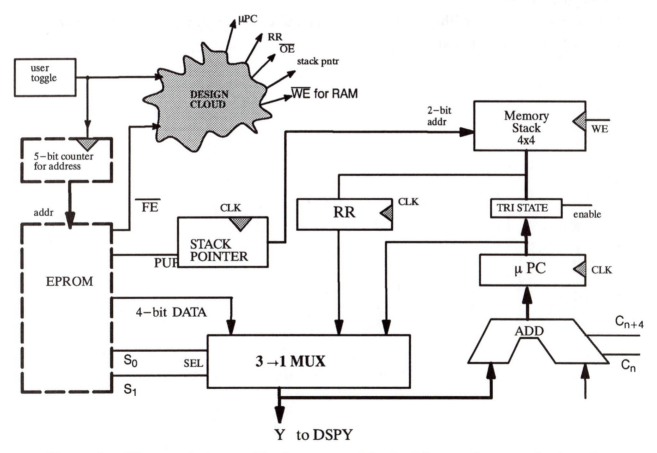

The major difference between this diagram and the text diagram for nested subroutines: The memory stack (2114) has common I/O pins, and must be buffered from the μPC by something like your LS240. You have to incorporate control of the '240 $\overline{OE}$ pin in your de-

Digital Design Lab Manual

sign and on your timing diagram. [You may want to waste your the 2nd 1−shot on your '123 insuring that the '240 $\overline{\text{OE}}$ stays low longer than the 2114 $\overline{\text{WE}}$.] The pipeline register RR looks out of place but really isn't, considering the arrangement of memory output. You would be foolish to use the 'LS373 for RR, because RR must be edge−triggered.

Discussion:

Lab C0 is the start of Lab C*. Add to your design for Lab C0 to build in the multiplexer, the ROM, the incrementer and the microprogram count register. Keep the SP display on your circuit for troubleshooting purposes. You will need to expand your controller circuit to include JUMP and JUMP−AND−POP instructions.

Specs and pinout for the 2909/2911, at the end of the Sata Sheet section, give more information you may need for this lab.

Possible FTQ's: We may ask at which step the sequencer test will fail if a given wire is pulled out of your circuit.

We may ask about some of the failed design attempts discussed in the supplementary material following this lab description.

TEST SEQUENCE FOR LAB C

ROM addr hex	Op Code Mnemonic	D−bus hex	$S_1 S_0 \overline{FE} PUP$	Expected Y bus
300	JUMP	0	1110	0
301	JUMP	1	1110	1
302	JUMP	2	1110	2
303	JUMP	4	1110	4
304	JUMP	8	1110	8
305	JUMP	F	1110	F
306	CONT	0	0011	10
307	CONT	0	0011	11
308	JUMP	6	1110	6
309	CONT	0	0011	7
30A	JSR	1	1101	1
30B	RTS	5	1000	8
30C	JSR	2	1101	2
30D	JSR	6	1101	6
30E	JSR	A	1101	A
30F	JSR	C	1101	C
310	CONT	0	0011	D
311	RTS	0	1000	B
312	RTS	0	1000	7
313	RTS	0	1000	3
314	RTS	0	1000	9
315	JSR	5	1101	5
316	JSR	3	1101	3
317	JPP	D	1100	D
318	RTS	0	1000	A

4 Tutorial for Lab C: Sequencing the Sequencer

Some of the following is a **design example** for the subroutine stack problem of Lab C*, as needed in Lab C0.

4.1 Microprogram instruction pipeline

Before we plunge into the design details of a sequencer's subroutining requirements, let's look at an "architectural" aspect of microprogramming—Speed increase through pipelining. Pay attention, because understanding a pipeline will be essential to the design example worked in this note; pipeline timing in particular will be important. Let's draw some timing diagrams and see what gets done when...we'll try to answer questions about how fast a string of commands for what−to−do−next can get out of microcode ROM and into the CPU. Shown below is a simplified microprogramming architecture, with one level of pipelining, which we developed in the text Chapters 7 & 11. Recall that with this architecture, the microcode must contain the Destination−branch for the **next** sequencer instruction.

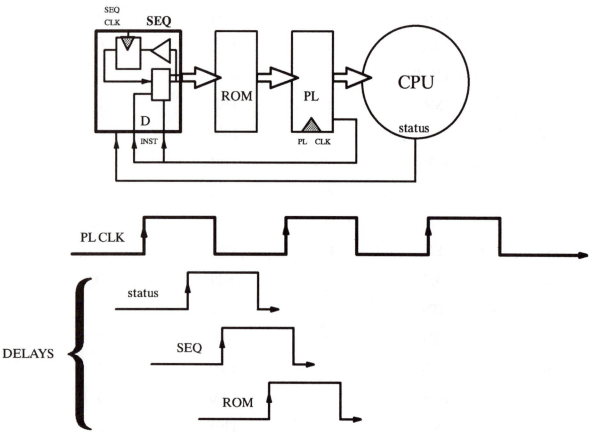

First note that if we *didn't* have the PL register—if the ROM attached directly to the CPU—we could have a *race condition* (see text chapter 5) if the SEQ instruction selected the D input. There would be nothing in the loop to stop data from racing around incrementing ROM addresses, thus the sequencer clock becomes necessary.

Now suppose the PL=pipeline register clock is rising−edge triggered; this means that a new instruction is presented to the CPU at the PL CLK arrows shown above, on the PL CLK line. How fast can we make these rising edges appear? We like to speed up until we ap−proach set−up and hold time violations for the flip flops in the pipeline register. Shown below PL CLK are the three elements which will delay the system's timing. The CPU status must be determined, the sequencer next address must be chosen, and the ROM must put out a new microcode. If the next PL clock occurs before these delays elapse, the next instruction won't be ready in time for the PL to latch it in.

Assume that the SEQ CLK = PL CLK, so that, during a plain *increment* sequencer instruc−tion, the sequencer updates in plenty of time. However, if the sequencer must wait for **status**, the worst−case delay ensues: all three of **status, sequencer, and microcode ROM** contribute to the loop delay.

Is there any way to speed up our sequencer as given? Here's an idea: Let's add two more pipe−line registers, for status and ROM addr, and see what happens:

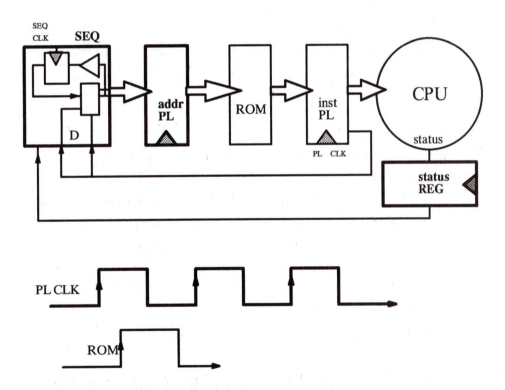

Now we latch in the *previous* status, and latch in the *next* address from the sequencer, so the PL register doesn't have to wait for either of those signals. The good news is that such an architecture can speed up the one−level pipelining by almost a factor of two; the bad news is that microprogramming becomes more complicated because the information in the PL register must contain sequencer information for **two** instructions in the future.

Digital Design Lab Manual

Simile for pipeline: an escalator carrying people from one floor to the next...slow, but much faster than one person at a time...

Master-Slave flip flop as an example of pipelining. recall Chpt 5.

    Notes on pipelining:
pipelining AN INSTRUCTION (see Sharp, p.25)
we've seen that the execution of one instruction can have several phases. Let's list the phases of TWO sequential instructions and inspect for how much overlap the two can have.
Assume the instructions are NOT branching types.
FRAME

        fetch
        execute
        inc prog cntr

    After a user instruction has been fetched, the microcode in ROM is latched in a register (now we know why AMD calls it the PL register!).Then after execution of the function in the ALU, results are stored in ACC and status is latched in another register. These three operations:

        fetch
        microcode
        execute/status

can be overlapped. While the microcode for the first instruction is being placed in the PL register, the next user instruction can be latched into the MAP register. Of course this assumes that status determined after the execution won't affect the next instruction selection (no branching).If conditional branching instructions are to be executed, then all bets are off.
FRAME for PL registers.
Without pipelining two instructions would take 6 clock cycles; with pipelining the instructions are finished in 4.

For further reading: chapter 5, "Microinstruction design," of G.J. Myers, *Digital System Design with LSI Bit−Slice Logic.* John Wiley & Sons, New York, 1980.

Digital Design Lab Manual

4.2 Emulation of 2911 sequencer

Emulation of the AMD2911 sequencer is our design problem. We'll mimic a subset of 2911 instructions. What follows will be a useful <u>case study</u> in designing a moderately complicated system. Notice, as you read along, how we keep sub-systems modular, as much as possible. We design and build one part, before moving on to the next, and parts are fairly independent of each other. We check our design on paper with a timing diagram; such checking reveals a few false steps along the way.

What we'll end up with works (at acceptably low clock rates), but is definitely not what AMD put on the 2911 chip. Our ultimate worry will be the design of a sequencer without a real clock...we'll have to time our pulses correctly, applying lessons learned in § 11.

4.2.1 Instructions to be emulated

We must account for five instructions:

	S_1	S_0	$\overline{FE}$	PUP
CONT= continue by increment	0	0	1	1
JUMP to D bus address	1	1	1	0
JSR = jump to subroutine	1	1	0	1
RTS = return from subroutine	1	0	0	0
JPP = jump & pop	1	1	0	0

which are announced on four output pins of a ROM, the other 4 being the DATA bits represent a jump address.

$S_1 S_0$ select inputs on a multiplexer; for example, $S_1 S_0 = 11$ selects the DATA bits.

PUP is a push/pop signal and controls whether the stack counter goes up or down; $\overline{FE}$ = file-enable-nought is active-low only when a memory stack is involved, in subroutine operations.

As you will see, the principle challenge of the design lies in the timing required to achieve the stack operations. Pay particular attention to design of the JSR and RTS operations. We will find it useful to draw out timing diagrams at each stage of the design.

First we need a <u>three-input</u> MUX, to provide the output. Data path is 4 bits wide. Let's say all we have available are two 2→1 MUX sets, one inverting (74158). Except for an overall inversion, this should do the trick [the '158 is an inverting MUX].

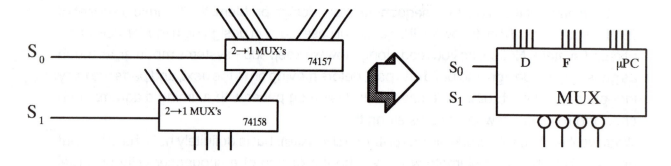

You've seen this figure before, in § 4. What annoyances would arise if the 157 and 158 MUX's were reversed in the diagram?

We want to make our 2911 operate quickly; this means we should probably avoid the extra delay of an output latch.

4.2.2 JUMP and table look–up sequencing

If we know in advance a particular sequence, then we can "solve" it entirely by table look–up, using only the JUMP instruction.

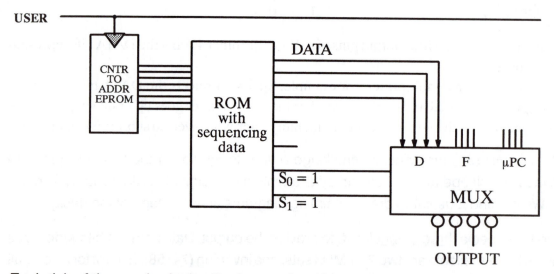

Each tick of the user's clock will advance the address counter to the next word or ROM, where the appropriate sequence number would be stored as DATA. For this, $S_1 S_0$ would always be programmed to 11.

However, we can't always know the sequence in advance. For example, we may have planned for an external interrupt by writing an interrupt service routine, but the exact time of the interrupt will be unknown to us, only the address of the interrupt's service routine.

Notice that the JUMP occurs immediately after the next ROM word appears; the only clocked element is the address counter:

Digital Design Lab Manual

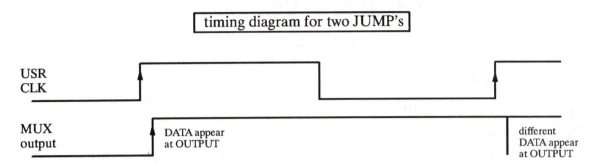

The delay from USR CLK to appearance of DATA at MUX output is due to propagation delay in the counter, and the ROM.

4.2.3 CONTINUE by increment

If, as part of a sequence, we want to go to the next larger binary number, then we can create a MUX pathway $S_1S_0 = 00$ which selects the output of the previous sequence number incremented by 1. This will be called the CONTINUE instruction.

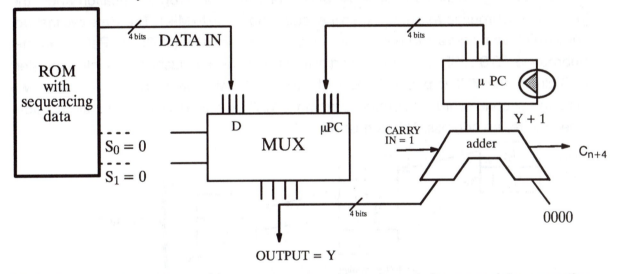

We're incrementing with an adder, not a counter, although we do have a register accepting adder output, like the accumulators you've seen before. As a consequence, there is a new clock point to control, the μPC clock (circled, above). When the ROM instruction $S_1S_0 = 00$ appears μPC inputs on the MUX will be selected immediately, so that had better be ready at the μPC register output. When should μPC be clocked? The USR CLK seems like a good choice, *if the μPC register is edge triggered*, as it should be.

Digital Design Lab Manual

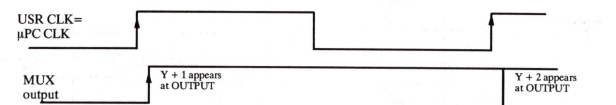

We call Y the output, so Y+1 is what we want after executing a CONT instruction. For a CONT instruction the DATA bits are don't−care's. In the exercises at the end of this § you can explore what would go wrong if the μPC clock were strobed *later* than USR CLK...you'd see Y+2 at the output...

4.2.4 One−level JUMP to subroutine

Jumping to a Subroutine is more involved than just JUMPing. Remember from the previous § that, after execution of a subroutine, the sequence must return to the main program where it left to go to the subroutine. Actually, if M is the main program location where the jump−to−subroutine was made, then the return should be to M+1. There are two instructions which complete a subroutine call: Jump−to−Subroutine (JSR) and Return−from−Subroutine (RTS). JSR jumps to the start of the subroutine <u>and</u> pushes M+1 into a register; RTS directs the MUX to pop M+1 out of the register. If, while we're in one subroutine, we jump to a second subroutine before returning to MAIN, we need a second location to store a second return address. This is **nesting.**

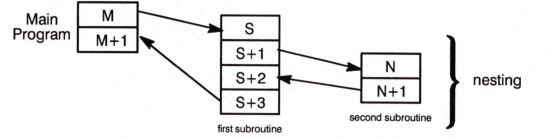

Let's add to our JUMP and CONT design a JSR, in one−level, un−nested, subroutining.

We need a storage register for the return address, M+1. M+1 should be available at the output of the incrementer, so let's try placing our second register on the same level as μPC.

Digital Design Lab Manual

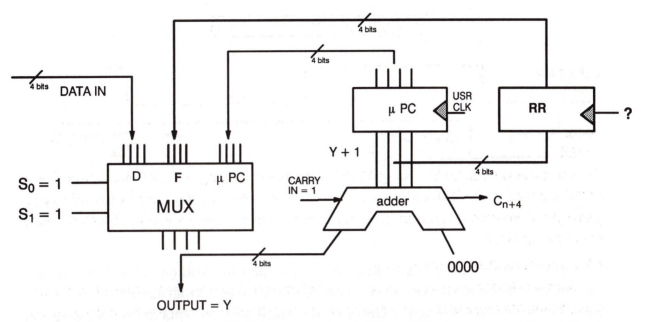

We're calling our new register "RR" (return register). Since JSR places the starting address of the subroutine on the output of the sequencer, it will use $S_1S_0 = 11$, like the JUMP instruction did. When the system is ready for RTS, the output of RR has its own path, F (for file) to the MUX. As long as we're **not** subroutining, RR can be clocked like μPC. But JSR must stop clocks to RR, so the address M+1 can be saved. Let's try this attempt to deal with control of RR clock:

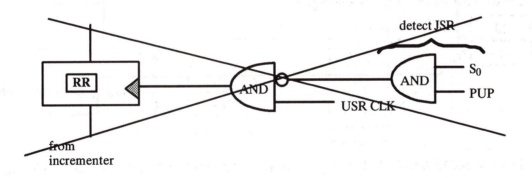

It's wrong, but heading in the right direction. It successfully detects the JSR instruction*
and tries to inhibit the RR clock. But this scheme will only last as long as the JSR instruction
is present. We need a longer lasting inhibition.

---

* Recall the instruction code for JSR = S1 S0 $\overline{\text{FE}}$ PUP $_=$ 1 1 0 1. JSR is the only one of the five
codes with S0 PUP $_=$ 1 1, so we can use that pattern to detect JSR.

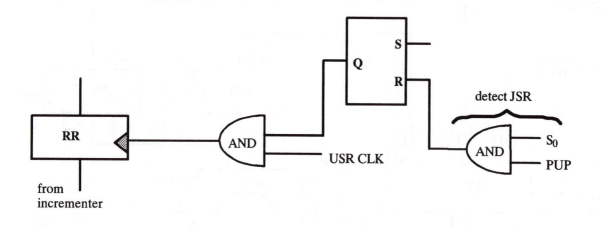

We use JSR–detect to reset a flip flop which will disable the AND gate. The AND gate will stay disabled until RTS occurs. RTS will then SET the flip flop. What about the timing? Will RR really latch in M+1? Yes. The USR CLK will beat the FF Q output to the AND gate and allow RR to latch the present value of the incrementer, which is M+1. The DATA, which has gone to the input of the incrementer, hasn't had time to take over the incrementer output. See diagrams below.

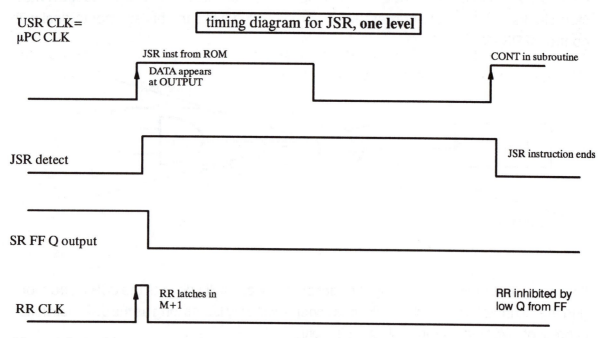

Note delays shown, to highlight duration of RR CLK.

4.2.5 Problems with Return from Subroutine, one–level

Instruction for RTS = S_1 S_0 $\overline{FE}$ PUP = 1 0 0 0.

As soon as RTS appears $S_1 S_0$ will expose the RR register value to the MUX output, which is the right thing to do, but RTS must also "pop" the RR clock, so a subsequent JSR can be

Digital Design Lab Manual

effective:

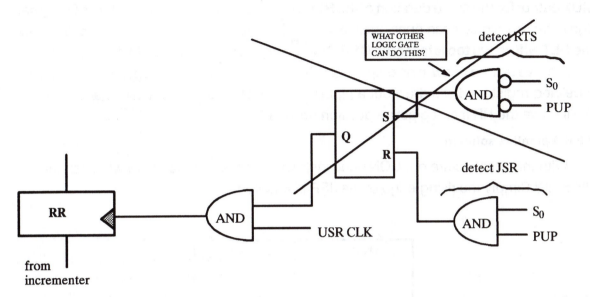

We can legally send our RTS−detect directly to the SR flip flop (since JSR and RTS will never occur simultaneously, we don't have to worry about the SR flip flop going into the not−allowed state of SR = 11). And because RTS "pops" the RR during the RTS instruction, but with some delay with respect to the USR CLK (exaggerated, in the figure above), RR is able to latch in **M+2**, the correct CONTINUE value for the next instruction. **But RR latches M+2 too soon, and F therefore changes before the RTS instruction is over. We need a way to delay the RTS strobe to RR.** Let's see if a delay tactic can work:

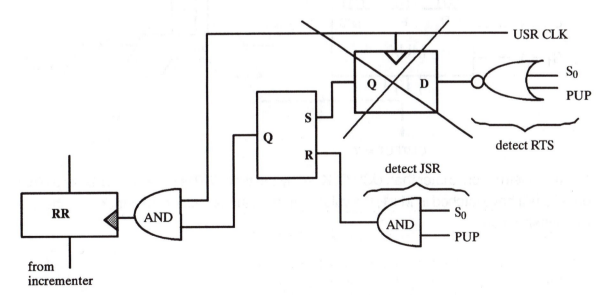

Our new delay element is an edge−triggered D−flip flop clocked by USR. Since detection of RTS must occur <u>after</u> USR clock, the D−flip flop won't send the RTS−detect signal across to the SET input until the start of the next instruction, after RR has had time to be the MUX output for the entire duration of the RTS instruction. When the SR flip flop is finally set again, the RR register can once again accept values from the incrementer. **Unfortunately the SET will arrive too late for the USR CLK to latch in the required M + 1.** It looks like we have to give up and throw in an output latch. But wait. What was the first part of this § about? Pipelined registers. Let's draw out a pipeline architecture and see what it can do for us. We'll move the RR into a pipeline position above µPC:

4.2.6 A pipeline solution

With this architecture our CONTinue instruction remains intact. Now what can trigger RR clock? Simply the rising edge of the JSR instruction.

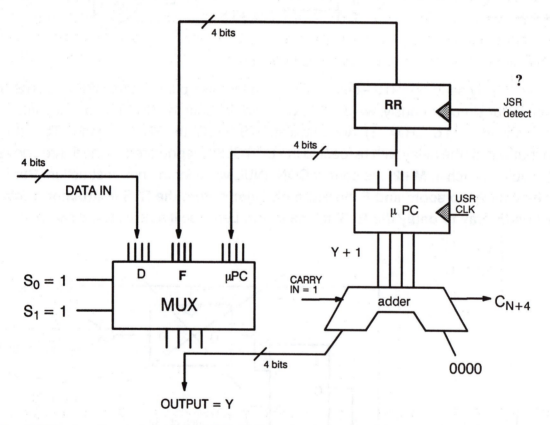

The JSR instruction is later than USR CLK, so by the time JSR is detected, USR as a clock on µPC will have latched in M+1, the value sitting on the output of the adder from the previous instruction.

See the timing diagram below:

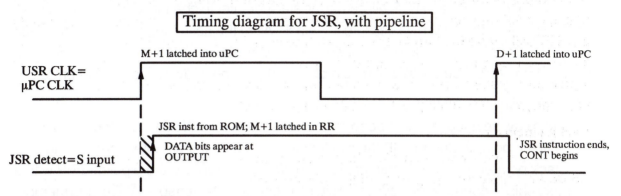

Timing diagram for JSR, with pipeline

And since we're concerned only with 1−level of it won't make sense to run 2 JSR's without an RTS in between. What about RTS? At the time RTS appears as an instruction, to select the F input to the MUX, the proper return address will be waiting and RTS won't have to clear RR, as it tried to do in our failed attempt above.

Look at the timing diagram again—How much delay is there between USR=μPC clock and JSR−detect=RR clock? (Cross−hatched zone) — The delay of counter plus ROM plus AND gate; if this total is greater than the set−up time of the RR register (and it easily should be), then we're done with a one−subroutine−level−deep sequencer.

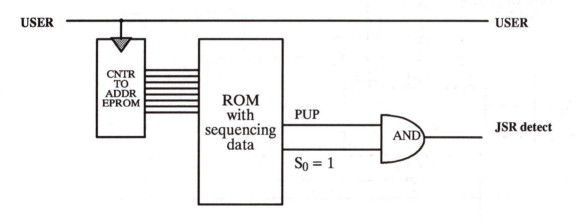

Pause, though, to look at the value of pipelining. The pipeline path created enough delay to allow the pipelined RR to receive the correct M+1 return address. Would this simple re−arrangement of clocks have solved the RR problem when RR was on the same level as μPC? No—in that case the incrementer faced RR input, and would have changed too quickly to let JSR detect be the RR clock.

Now on to **nesting**.

WHAT ABOUT JPP INSTRUCTION?

4.3 Adding a stack for nesting

To nest subroutines, we must be able to save more than one return address. We need a small SRAM Last In, First Out (LIFO) stack, and its address generator (an up–down counter, or stack pointer). Both JSR and RTS will cause the stack pointer to change and JSR must evoke some way of <u>writing</u> return values into the stack. All of the action for controlling the stack must take place in one clock cycle, but we have only the rising and falling edges of the clock to start with. What you will see here is a bit of asynchronous design for stack control.

4.3.1 A stack, and its pointer

Let's say we need to nest 4 deep; that means we need 4 SRAM stack locations and a 2–bit stack pointer. During JSR the stack pointer must be incremented, and during RTS the stack pointer must be decremented. Can we simply replace the pipelined RR with a memory chip + counter? We have three sites to control: write–enable=$\overline{WE}$ on the memory stack, Up/down on the stack pointer, and stack pointer clock.

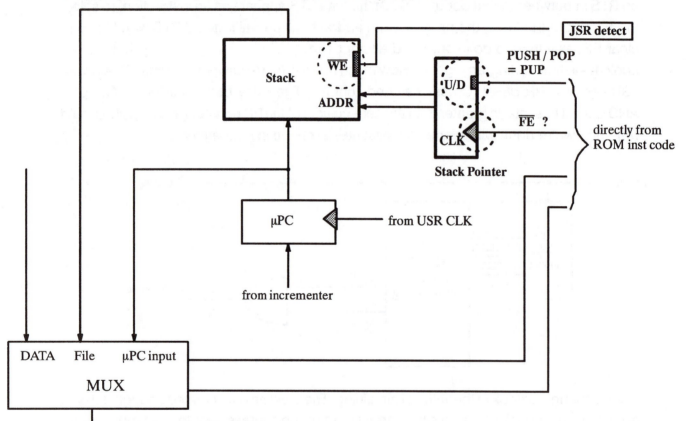

The only time we'd want to write to the stack would be during a JSR instruction, so let's think about connecting $\overline{WE}$ directly to JSR (which we may have to decode...see JSR detect signal above). Direct connect of JSR–detect to $\overline{WE}$ may be a problem because write in a SRAM is a level–sensitive, not edge–sensitive input; whatever is the data for the address given *when $\overline{WE}$ goes HI again will be written on the stack.* You may need a 1–shot to create a <u>pulse</u> for $\overline{WE}$.

Digital Design Lab Manual

The ROM code for the instructions has an output PUP = push/pop which, as it looks from the instruction codes, can go straight to up/down control on the counter (arrival of PUP at the counter will be delayed from the USR clock by the ROM. The instruction set also has a variable $\overline{FE}$, which we haven't used up to now and which is active–low only during JSR and RTS. Can $\overline{FE}$ go directly to stack clock? No, it must be AND'd with USR CLK in order to produce new edges for consecutive JSR's or RTS's. *But because PUP comes delayed off the ROM with respect to $\overline{FE}$, we need to delay the counter clock to wait for PUP.* Try ANDing $\overline{FE} \cdot \overline{USR}$ (what does DeMorgan's Law say about that expression?). See timing diagram below.

4.3.2 JSR timing diagram for nesting stack

We haven't tampered with our hardware for JUMP and CONT instructions, so the timing for them must still be OK. Let's draw out JSR timing, with a 1–shot in the $\overline{WE}$ pathway. Keep in mind that when the inevitable RTS instruction arrives, we want the correct return address sitting on the output of the stack; that means we need to decrement before RR clock during RTS! Let's go through the timing diagram below:
USR is the user toggle switch, and it goes to the mPC to latch the increment of Y.
USR also increments the ROM address so with some delay a new instruction appears out of ROM. If the instruction is JSR, detect it and have it create a 1–shot pulse which goes to both write–enable of the SRAM and enable of the 3–state buffer facing the SRAM. Assume zero hold time will allow SRAM to grab correct value off of buffer. If JSR is the instruction let the stack pointer increment **after** the RR is clocked, so the RR holds the previous value. Let the RR clock be from a longer 1–shot which is gated by $\overline{FE}$ and USR (in case of continuous series of RTS). Since the last JSR has ended up pointing at the next stack address, an RTS must decrement **before** the RR clock; that way RR will bring in the correct stack position and will feed the MUX with the correct return address. As shown there may be a msec or so when an incorrect return address is shown, but you won't see it in your display.

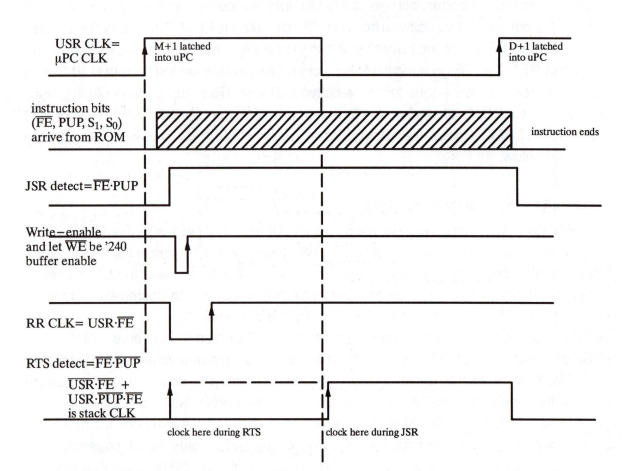

This timing looks good.

Here's the hardware:

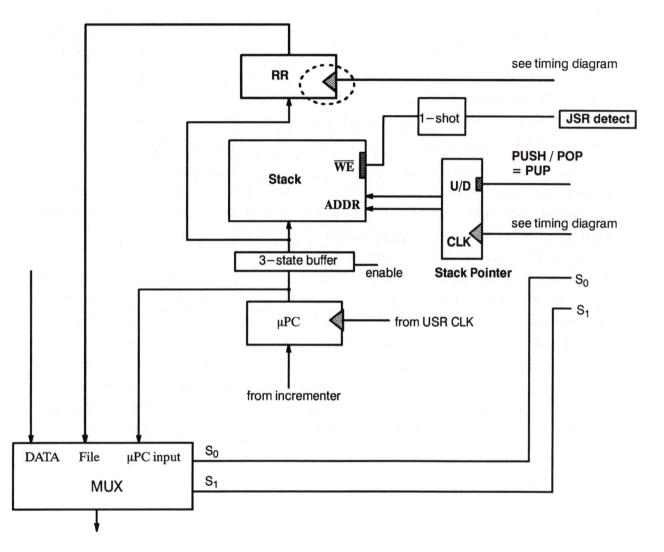

For the whole duration of the JSR instruction the jump location, DATA, will appear at the MUX output, and M+1 will be written into the stack. Let's worry for a moment about $\overline{FE}$ and PUP (clock and up/down control to the counter) being simultaneous. The data sheet for a chip like the 74169 says the set−up time for up/down is 30 ns. To play it safe we could delay the counter clock signal through 2 inverters. If we passed the counter clock (=$\overline{FE}$) through one inverter, it would be delayed until the middle of the cycle, and we would have to arrange a corresponding delay of the WE signal for RAM.

4.3.3 Another pipeline register for RTS

Now let's check what happens on RTS. Right away we see a problem, one that vexed us even in the one−level design: As soon as the stack pointer is decremented for RTS the stack output will change, and a different value will appear at F, before its time. Let's not re-peat the failed attempts to delay RTS stack pointer clock. Instead we know to go right ahead and add another level to our pipeline:

The question: What should control the clock to our newly−installed return register, RR? Here's what we want to have happen in the pipeline—(1) μPC latches M+1 (2) M+1 is writ-ten into stack (3) contents of stack is transferred to return register before stack pointer changes. We already have clock signals for (1) and (2). We could, with 1−shots, rig up a third, delayed, pulse for RR during JSR, but instead, consider this: Once (1) and (2) are done during a JSR, we're in no rush to write the stack output to RR. We can wait until the next USR CLK. In fact if USR CLK is the clock signal for RR, we'll be OK. That just means at the start of every cycle we save the stack on RR. Our final design looks like this:

Digital Design Lab Manual

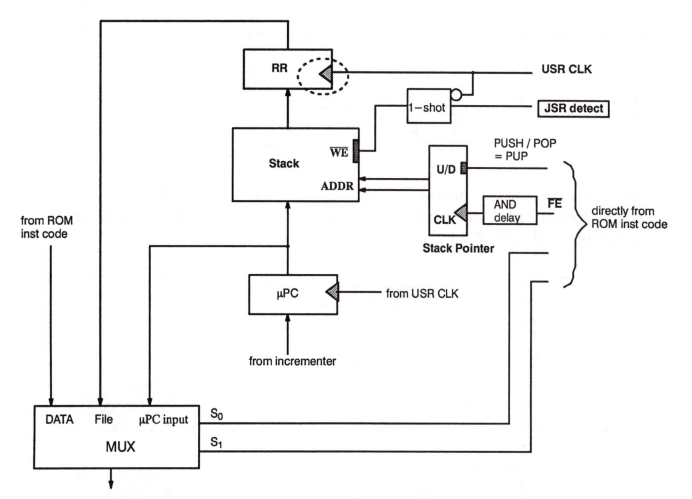

The FE for stack pointer clock should be AND'd with USR CLK so that a consecutive string of JSR's or RTS's will still provide <u>edges</u> for the SP counter input. And $\overline{USR}$ should gate the JSR write pulse, as explained below.

7/27/90: built it; it works!

Suppressing an unwanted WE pulse when RTS follows JSR.

One way to detect a JSR instruction: **$\overline{FE}$ PUP = 0 1.** On a typical static RAM chip write−enable is active−low. Let's use the 74123 1−shot for $\overline{WE}$ on the RAM. $\overline{WE}$ should go low only during a JSR instruction. *However, if USR CLK gates JSR to produce a $\overline{WE}$ pulse, everything will work correctly* except *an RTS after JSR. In that case another rising USR edge will occur <u>before</u> JSR terminates, causing an unwanted write pulse to memory at the start of RTS.*

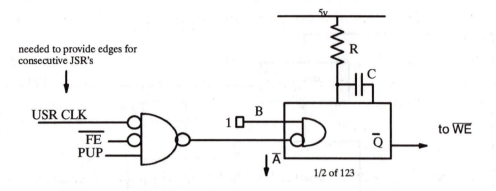

[50KΩ is maximum value for R. The product R · C = τ determines the duration of the $\overline{WE}$ pulse.]

Since there is no rush to write to memory during a cycle, we can **delay the write pulse** until the low phase of the USR clock. See timing below.

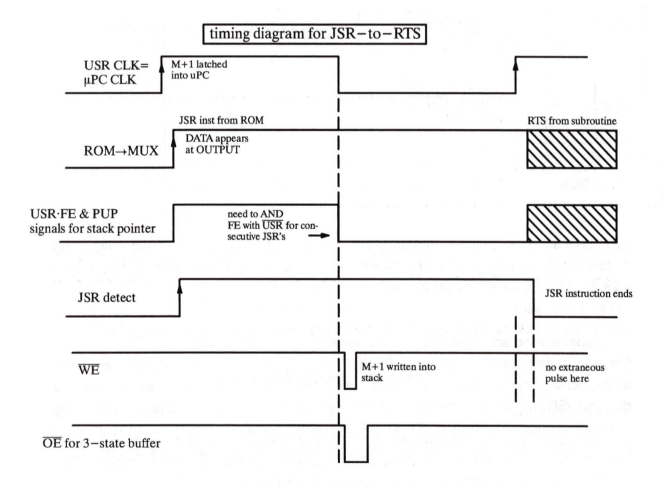

Digital Design Lab Manual

NOTE: may need to use $\overline{\text{USR}}$ gated with $\overline{\text{FE}}$ as the stack clock because $\overline{\text{FE}}$ will be continuously LO and the clock will beat the PUP control to the stack pointer.

JSR RTS JSR results in SRAM address going 0 1 2 instead of 0 1 0. FE is always low for subroutine instructions. Can make a 3 bit counter to SRAM and see 0 1 2 1 2 3 4 3 2 1 on the SRAM address. Can try extra delay on stack clock.

Do you need an async re-design? Follow through on Lab C0!

The RTS timing diagram requires the addition of RR clk. For clarity, let's just show the timing in the pipeline, for RTS:

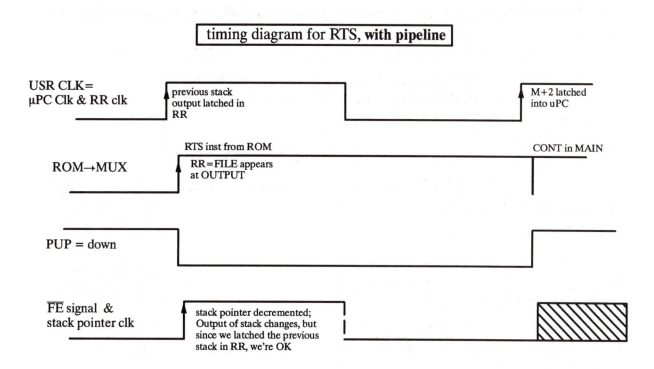

timing diagram for RTS, **with pipeline**

USR CLK=
μPC Clk & RR clk

previous stack output latched in RR

M+2 latched into uPC

RTS inst from ROM

CONT in MAIN

ROM→MUX

RR=FILE appears at OUTPUT

PUP = down

$\overline{\text{FE}}$ signal &
stack pointer clk

stack pointer decremented; Output of stack changes, but since we latched the previous stack in RR, we're OK

No write−enable pulse should occur during RTS, even immediately after a JSR.

4.4 Conclusion

We've finished a successful design of a nesting sequencer, using the idea of pipelining to solve many of our timing problems. Of course there are other "architectures" which will work to interpret correctly the sequencer instruction set.*

The main point about our design: How to generate a sequence of operations with only the rising edge of USR clock as a starting event. No other clock pulses came along. With the pipeline approach, we were able to design a solution without any hidden clocks, only 1–shot, and no output latches—annoyances which would have slowed down our system and made it more susceptible to timing problems. We have added to our skills by solving challenging timing problems.

At any rate, we truly have penetrated to the inner core of a micro–programmed computer. We tamed the rough beast of the sequencer. Let's recapitulate, peeling layers off the onion:

- A user's instruction tells the microprogram hardware what location in ROM starts the sequential execution of the instruction.
- As the user's instruction is being executed, micro–instruction by micro–instruction, part of each micro–instruction tells a sequencer which ROM address to select next.
- The sequencer can select, with a MUX, between (1) DATA from the micro–instruction, (2) an incremental continuation, (3) return from a subroutine.
- Subroutine return locations are stored on a *stack*, addressed by a stack pointer.

4.5 Summary

★ **Pipeline registers** increase sequencer/CPU speed by allowing selection of next instruction **while** the current one is being executed.

★ A multiplexer selects the next ROM address, whose contents guide CPU source, function, destination and next instruction.

★ Jump–To–Subroutine requires that a return address be stored on a stack.

★ ReTurn–from–Subroutine requires that the previously stored return address be popped off the stack.

★ A 3–level pipeline architecture satisfies the requirements for a nested–subroutine sequencer; hardware and timing diagrams are worked out.

---

* For example, it's possible to place the incrementer like this:

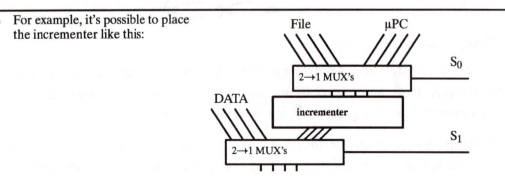

Digital Design Lab Manual

Lab D

D   Traffic Light Square Dance

Requirements.

Think about an intersection where a secondary one-way road crosses a highway. There are <u>three</u> inductive loop vehicle sensors, and pedestrian buttons as input, and possibly a 2 second timer.
Outputs are the R-Y-G traffic lights and pedestrian
WALK/DON'T WALK signs.
If there has been no traffic for over a minute, then the main highway light is always green. When a car pulls up to the one-way cross street the lights will go through a yellow-red sequence of stopping the main highway and making green the one-way light. The one-way cross street can be green as long as 30 seconds, then the main highway gets to go again, and can be on for 30 seconds in case a second car has pulled up to the one-way street. If a pedestrian pushes a WALK button at any of the 4 corners then a sequence is started to stop <u>both</u> directions of traffic so pedestrians can "square dance" catty corner across the intersection if they like.

Devise a finite state machine to implement the traffic light controller and use software to compile your state design and fit it into a 22V10 PAL. *If the PAL programmer is down, go ahead and implement the design in LogicWorks.*

See chapter 7 of *Digital Design from Zero to One.*

Lab E

E   Elevator Controller

Requirements:

Make a circuit to control a freight elevator (like the one in the
Shop Building). The heart of your controller will be a finite
state machine (FSM). Inputs to your FSM: CALL buttons on the wall
of basement and ground; B and G buttons inside the car; manual
DOOR CLOSE button inside the car; shaft detectors for car at B or
G locations (if neither detector is asserted, then the car is
assumed to be between floors). Outputs of your FSM: Motor ON-OFF
for car & Motor for car UP-DOWN; DOOR closer MOTOR; DOOR opener
MOTOR.

To simulate the elevator car movement, have the motor controls go
to a counter chip to control counter enable (ON-OFF) and direction of counter. Display the count so we can see where the elevator car is. The shaft detectors will be comparators which test
the counter output with the B and G thresholds.

Let the clock to the counter be slow enough to make movement of
the elevator seem realistic.

For no FTQ, make a controller for a **3-floor elevator.**
Display what floor the car is on.

You can do the elevator controller either by simulation in LogicWorks or Beige Bag, or by
programming a 22V10. Use the MOORE MACHINE feature of PALASM to have the program compile the excitation equations for the flip flops in the PAL.

For more insight, go ride a freight elevator; they usually have more manual control than a
passenger elevator. Elevator controllers like this one are standard fare for projects in Don
Troxel's 6.111 EECS course at MIT.

An elevator controller is featured in chapter 7 of *Digital Design from Zero to One.*
At some point we will make a model elevator and shaft out of LEGO bricks and LEGO mo-
tors, and watch the whole operation in real time!

Lab CPU

This is a challenging lab...and by 1995 the original 2901 was no longer supported by AMD. Try this lab at your own risk. It is becoming obsolete!

CPU   4—Bit Central Processing Unit

Requirements. Build a 4-bit CPU which executes the following instruction set:

Mnemonic	Recursive Definition
NOP	$ACC \leftarrow ACC$
INV	$ACC \leftarrow \overline{ACC}$
SHIFT UP	$ACC \leftarrow ACC$ plus ACC
LDI	$ACC \leftarrow DB$
LOAD	$ACC \leftarrow RAM$
STORE	$RAM \leftarrow ACC$
ADD	$ACC \leftarrow ACC$ plus RAM
SUB	$ACC \leftarrow ACC$ minus RAM
AND	$ACC \leftarrow ACC \wedge RAM$
OR	$ACC \leftarrow ACC \vee RAM$
ADDI	$ACC \leftarrow ACC$ plus DB
SUBI	$ACC \leftarrow ACC$ minus DB
ANDI	$ACC \leftarrow ACC \wedge DB$
ORI	$ACC \leftarrow ACC \vee DB$
JMPZ	$PC \leftarrow 0$
JIFZ	$PC \leftarrow 0$ only if $ACC = 0$

ACC = accumulator
PC = program counter
RAM = location in **internal** memory stack
DB = external data bits
minus & *plus* are **arithmetic** operations; $\wedge$ & $\vee$ are **logical** (bit-by-bit) operations.

In your circuit to be checked off, have a toggle—activated counter address an EPROM which contains the test program. Display the ACC and PC. Have a **status light** for carry—out.

Digital Design Lab Manual

Each instruction must be *two bytes* long, in one of the following formats
(for the 74181 or 74LS382):

BYTE 0 (even)	MUX	$\overline{WE}$	C_{in}	M	S_3	S_2	S_1	S_0
BYTE 1 (odd)	DB_3	DB_2	DB_1	DB_0	RAM_θ	RAM_2	RAM_1	RAM_0

MUX determines whether RAM or the data bus (DB) has access to the ALU.
in the code below we'll use the convention that MUX=0 selects DB's.
The data bits should go into the B inputs of the 181/382.

$\overline{WE}$ is *write enable active low* for the scratchpad RAM.

Each DB_i is an *immediate* data bit.

RAM_i 's are address bits for the local scratchpad.

C_{in}, M, and S_i are 74181 control signals.

The 74181 can perform 32 different functions, only a few of which will be useful to us. The 382 has fewer, but more normal functions. We'll use the convention for JUMP described in §21 of the text, where MUX, $\overline{WE}$ = 1 0 is used to represent a JUMP. ACC should route back to A input pins for the INVERT code in the table below.

(for the 2901):

	MSB OF EPROM							
BYTE 0 (even)	I_0	I_1	I_2	I_3	I_4	I_5	I_6	I_7
BYTE 1 (odd)	I_8	C_{in}	D_3	D_2	D_1	D_0	$A-B_1$	$A-B_0$

"A−B" refers to two address pins on the 2901, both A and B ports. Ground the other address pins.

D_i are the data bits, which have direct access to pins on the 2901.

Including C_{in}, there are 10 instruction bits for the 2901, so the 2901 clock pulse will have to wait until the second byte is present before the ALU result is correct and the DESTINATION can be secure.

Using the 2901, we will access only 4 of the 16 RAM locations.

You also have the Q−register available as an internal "accumulator."

In the EPROM code for the 2901 the unused EXOR instruction will be used to signal a JUMP−IF−ZERO.

Look over supplemental text chapter S5 on microprogramming before starting lab CPU.

Test your CPU using a DIP switch to enter both bytes of the instruction. When the LSB of the PC is '0', the DIP switch settings represent the BYTE 0 or *op—code*; when the LSB is '1', the switch represents the BYTE 1 or *source/destination code*.
Have a single—step clock = toggle switch drive the program counter.
You'll need to draw out a timing diagram to know when ACC & IR should be latched.
For de—bugging, *you the student* play the role of program and data memory by reading the odd or even value off the PC display and manually changing the DIP switch settings to the desired instruction! (For checking off, we will provide you with an EPROM containing a series of instructions, you can hook up a counter to EPROM; during the execution of the program the counter value is displayed, and returns to 0 when a JUMP is executed.)

First decision: 181/382— or 2901—based system? Pick the 2901——you have 40 pins to hook up, on one chip, but fewer ancillary chips to go around.

[181. If the '181 is you choice, then pick appropriate chips for the ancillary registers, memory and multiplexers. What 4 bit parallel load chip can function as **accumulator**? As with the 2901 you will need an **8—bit instruction register** (IR) which latches BYTE 0. Study how to adapt your memory chip to the role of "internal" scratch pad (cache memory); you'll only need at most 4 address pins..the other address pins can be tied low. How can the RAM I/O multiplex with the ACC output? You could use a tri—state buffer between ACC and RAM. You may need <u>three</u> MUX's, including the 74158, to complete the design: one for display MUX, one for RAM/DB MUX and one tri—state for ACC/RAM MUX (be careful about inversion if you use the LS240).

For the 181, your main design problem is the control circuit required to manipulate the latches of ACC and IR, interpret the LSB of the PC, route data through the multiplexer and RAM, and achieve PC JUMP changes.]

2901. For the 2901 we'll use the Q register as the accumulator.
Study the data sheet paragraph which explains the actions of the clock, on both Q and RAM. The RAM on the 2901, like the other static RAM we've studied, has a level—sensitive active—low write—enable; it can be written to when clock is low—it's not edge triggered. You may want to put a 1—shot, with $\overline{Q}$ as output, between your regular 2—phase clock for the 2901 and the 2901 clock pin; this will ensure that the 2901 clock is nearly always high, and RAM will be protected from inadvertent writing. We need to do this because the instruction is **9** bits long and we latch in only the first 8 bits on the first clock pulse; this can leave an arbitrary 9th bit acting with the first 8 bits, and if you happen to make a RAM write destination with the arbitrary 9th bit, the low clock will allow it in, even though you don't want it.

To verify your CPU's operation, we will ask you to execute various instructions as we watch the ACC and PC change. You should have a **single-step clock** for moving through sequential even and odd counts.

(1993) **Shifting on 2901:** Are the codes for RAMQ shift up and shift down correct or reversed? Test by hardwiring in a shift instruction and looking to see whether shift up fills in data to the left, and vice versa for shift down. Be sure to account for Q_0 Q_3 RAM_3 RAM_0.

You can troubleshoot your circuit with an 8-bit DIP switch, but for checking off we'll want to insert a counter-addressed EPROM, and step through the code shown below.

Addressing the EPROM. For the 181 ALU, code starts at EPROM address 0000; for the 2901 code starts at address 0100. 74181—tie all higher order address bits low. 2901—tie EPROM address A_8 high, and the other higher order address on the EPROM low in order to access the 2901 codes 01XX.
You should tie the unused 2901 RAM addresses low so you're certain which locations your 2nd byte of instruction accesses.

Codes in EPROM for the 2901 versions of lab CPU:

2901 EPROM CODE

X = 0 in the EPROM

[the 1XX address is shown **above** each hex contents]

INST	DATA	SOURCE $I_0I_1I_2$	FUNC $I_3 I_4 I_5$	DEST $I_6 I_7\ I_8$	Cin	DATA	RAM	EPROM ADDR HEX CODE	Y BUS
							ADDRESS =	100 101	
LDI	7	1 1 1	1 1 0	0 0 0	X	01 11	XX	F8 1C	7
							ADDRESS =	102 103	
STORE in 11		0 1 0	1 1 0	0 1 0	X	XXXX	11	59 03	7
							ADDRESS =	104 105	
LDI	E	1 1 1	1 1 0	0 0 0	X	11 10	XX	F8 38	E
							ADDRESS =	106 107	
STORE in 00		0 1 0	1 1 0	0 1 0	X	XXXX	00	59 00	?
							ADDRESS =	108 109	
AND	RAM	0 0 0	0 0 1	0 0 0	X	XXXX	11	04 03	6
							ADDRESS =	10A 10B	
SHIFT UP		0 1 0	1 1 0	0 1 1	X	XXXX	00	59 80	6
							ADDRESS =	10C 10D	
NOP		0 1 0	0 0 0	0 0 0	0	XXXX	XX	40 00	C
							ADDRESS =	10E 10F	
INVERT		0 1 0	1 1 1	0 0 0	X	00 00	XX	5C 00	3
							ADDRESS =	110 111	
NOP		0 1 0	0 0 0	0 0 0	0	XXXX	XX	40 00	3
							ADDRESS =	112 113	
ADI	5	0 1 1	0 0 0	0 0 0	0	01 01	XX	60 14	8
							ADDRESS =	114 115	
NOP		0 1 0	0 0 0	0 0 0	0	XXXX	XX	40 00	8
							ADDRESS =	116 117	
SUB	RAM	0 0 0	1 0 0	0 0 0	1	XXXX	00	10 40	?
							ADDRESS =	118 119	
NOP		0 1 0	0 0 0	0 0 0	0	XXXX	XX	40 00	?
							ADDRESS =	11A 11B	
ORI	3	0 1 1	1 1 0	0 0 0	X	00 11	XX	78 0C	?
							ADDRESS =	11C 11D	
SUBI	7	0 1 1	1 0 0	0 0 0	1	01 11	XX	70 5C	?
							ADDRESS =	11E 11F	
JMPD		1 0 0	**0** 1 1	0 0 0	X	01 00	XX	8C 10	?

above JUMPS to 14

CF808?

Digital Design Lab Manual

The instruction bits are listed from I₀ on the left to I₈ on the right, in source—function—destination fields. In the 2901 data sheets the ascending numbers are *right to left* for each field. **JUMP:** After detecting the final zero and jumping to location 0100, the process will start over. Notice that, at the end, you'll need to detect function code 011 and Y=0000 in order to "load" the EPROM—addressing counter with the specified data.

There are 32 locations to address, so you'll need a 5th bit to complete the job; have the 5th bit light an LED. On your 7433 we'll see the least significant hex digit of the current address, and the Y—bus output. **Is the Y bus value shown in the table correct before or after the 2901 clock?** What goes in place of ?'s? Do we have Carry—In right for 2's complement subtract? Maybe you should latch the display in time with the 2901 clock (effectively bring Q out to a 195 hooked to display), that way the display will change only once every two address changes. You will want to bypass the display latch for troubleshooting. We'll only care about what's on the Y—bus for ODD address, although what the system does on even address may provide you troubleshooting information. Figure out what goes where there are question marks above. Make sure your system gives the same answers over and over to the ROM code; if it doesn't maybe you haven't tied *all* inputs to *something*, or maybe the power lines don't have adequate bypass.

More troubleshooting the 2901: Be able to stop toggle pulses to the address generator counter and the address latch, but still allow clock pulses to the 2901. That way you can stop at an instruction address you think is giving a wrong answer and watch what the instruction executes over and over. For example, one student couldn't get the right answer at the step where ADD 5 occurs, and found that the system was adding A = 2x5, meaning that during his operation, **two** clock pulses got to the 2901 on <u>one</u> instruction cycle.

Bonus: Can you think of a way to implement a PC ← RAM or PC ← DB jump statement?

Power requirements. Depending on which chips you use in your design, your circuit may require quite a bit of current. If things don't seem to be going right, check with a voltmeter that you have $V_{CC} > 4.75$ volts. If you don't, switch to a larger power supply. According to its data sheet, the 2901 consumes 250 mA; it will feel warm to the touch.

Possible FTQ's: We may tie one of the data—in bits high or low and ask you what will appear on the ACC / Y—bus display as we step through the code. Or we may ask what will happen if the JIFZ counter—clear is disabled and the machine is forced to step into higher addresses. Other questions: What will appear on the ACC / Y—bus if one of the instructions bits is tied high or low and the system clocked twice? What if carry—in is tied high?

74181 EPROM CODE

X = 0 in the EPROM
[the 0XX address is shown above each hex contents]

INST	Data	MUX	WE	Cin M	FUNC	DB 3−0	ADDR 3−0	EPROM ADDR HEX CODE	ACC
							ADDRESS =	000 001	
LDI	5	0	1	0 1	1 0 1 0	0101	XXXX	5A 50	5
							ADDRESS =	002 003	
STORE		0	0	X X	1 1 1 1	XXXX	1100	0F 0C	5
							ADDRESS =	004 005	
AND RAM		1	1	X 1	1 0 1 1	XXXX	1100	DB 0C	5
							ADDRESS =	006 007	
SHIFT UP		1	1	1 0	1 1 0 0	XXXX	XXXX	EC 00	A
							ADDRESS =	008 009	
INVERT		1	1	X 1	0 0 0 0	XXXX	XXXX	D0 00	5
							ADDRESS =	00A 00B	
ADI	5	0	1	1 0	1 0 0 1	0101	XXXX	69 50	A
							ADDRESS =	00C 00D	
SUB RAM		1	1	1 0	0 1 1 0	XXXX	1100	E6 0C	4?
							ADDRESS =	00E 00F	
ORI	2	0	1	X 1	1 1 1 0	0010	XXXX	5E 20	6
							ADDRESS =	010 011	
SUBI	5	0	1	1 0	0 1 1 0	0101	XXXX	66 50	0
							ADDRESS =	012 013	
JIFZ		**1**	**0**	X X	1 1 1 1	XXXX	XXXX	8F 00	0

181 notes. Are "subtract" answers correct? When you use the EPROM, you don't have to demonstrate every instruction, just the ones in the above program. When you reach the last line, the program should jump back to the beginning. Notice that during the STORE instruction both Cin and M are zero...your system must take these values into account.

5 NOTES FOR CPU LAB

5 . 1 A CPU with the 181 as ALU

Consider the following schematic:

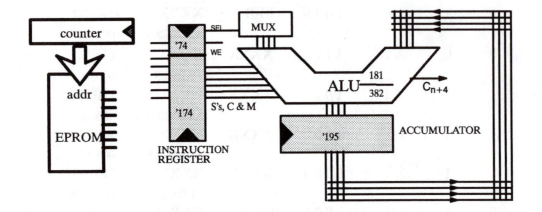

The 8–bit instruction from the EPROM is latched into the instruction register. Six of the 8 bits can project directly to the 181, the other two bits can be used for the input MUX and a memory write–enable. A 4–bit register can be the accumulator, which then feeds back to one of the ALU inputs.

Note that we're building a CPU with a 4–bit data path, but with an 8+8 instruction path!

Your DIP SWITCH can be used in place of EPROM to test the system by hand.

Now let's look at the signals to the input MUX.

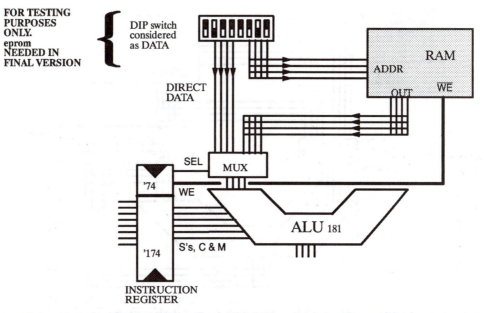

FOR TESTING PURPOSES ONLY.
eprom NEEDED IN FINAL VERSION

DIP switch considered as DATA

DIRECT DATA

RAM
ADDR
OUT
WE

SEL
MUX
WE

'74

'174   S's, C & M

ALU 181

INSTRUCTION REGISTER

One 4−bit input is immediate data from the DIP switch in the data mode; the other input is contents of scratchpad RAM, residing in the CPU. Of course in the final version you won't have a DIP−switch, you'll make direct connections to the EPROM.

Sometimes (such as during STORE) the ACC needs to go to the RAM data input. Let's involve a 3−state buffer to help out. Does the buffer need to be a register? No. The 3−state buffer is only enabled when the ACC must go to RAM, and in fact is only needed because we're dealing with a RAM which has IN & OUT on the same pins. The RAM serves as the "flip flops" for the storage operation. The buffer *could* be a register; then we would have to deal with the increased timing burden of the register's clock...

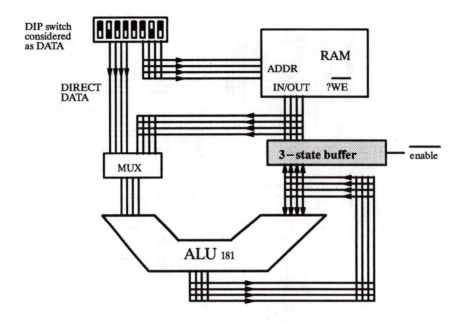

This gives us another pin—'240 enable—to control, but it should be related to the STORE = write instruction...Note also that the 'LS 240 is an **inverting** buffer, so what's written in is the complement of what was sent from ACC.

Let's review what needs to be controlled by the instruction:

181      $S_0 - S_3$
             C_n
             M
Input MUX
Write–enable on RAM
'240 enable
Instr. Reg. Clock
ACC Clock

What do we have available to do the controlling?

First of all, we've got the LSB of the program counter...let's put that in:

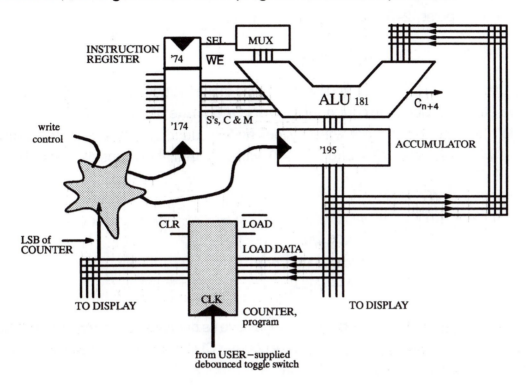

Let's draw out a possible timing diagram for this system:

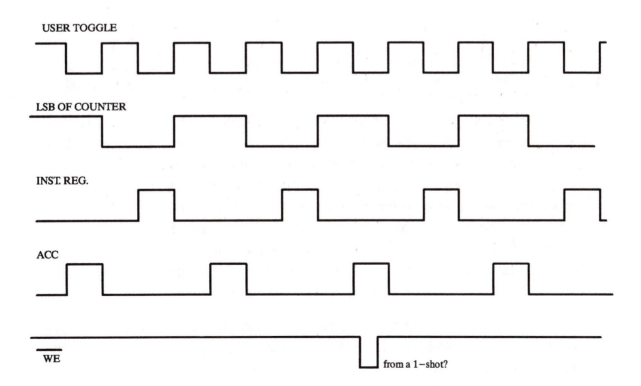

From these relationships in time you should be able to fill in the *DESIGN CLOUD*, including the proper write pulse/'240 enable signal hardware.

```
try SYNCHRONOUS DESIGN for the clock signals...
```

One last problem for the 181 approach: How to make the computer **JUMP**. Seems like we need a 9th instruction bit to control the CLR or LOAD on the COUNTER. Perhaps we can "make up" the necessary control signal by looking for redundancy in some of the instructions. If MUX = 0 selects DATA, and $\overline{WE}$ = 0 writes to RAM, then consider this scheme:

MUX	$\overline{WE}$	
0	0	ACC→RAM (perhaps by ADDing DATA=0 to ACC)
0	1	DATA→ALU
1	0	**redundant code**
1	1	RAM→ALU

Detect (with an AND gate?) the redundant code and have its detection represent JUMP; when the AND gate finds MUX, $\overline{WE}$ = 1 0, strobe the counter CLR. That's one possibility, anyway. Do you need to suppress writing to RAM in the JUMP case?

5 . 2 The 2901 in a CPU

Review the 2901 data sheets and pay attention to clock information. Pay attention to the 2901 clock attributes. All the time 2901 clock is LOW, data can be written to RAM.

A 2901 needs **9** instruction bits **and** a C_n carry-in bit. Since you'll use either an 8 bit DIP or an 8 bit ROM, you need to spread the 10 instruction bits over two address-counter clock cycles. On the 2nd byte you need to supply the 4-bit data input; as a consequence, only 2 bits are left in the 2nd byte for addressing the internal RAM on the 2901. But $2^2=4$ RAM locations should be enough for a small test program. The CPU requirements give a protocol for labeling the two bytes of information for the 2901. This protocol will be used in the EPROM supplied with 2901 code, which we can use for testing your design. At any rate, the 2901 needs an instruction register, but doesn't need an external accumulator, and doesn't need external RAM, or external data multiplexing, like the '181 design needed.

The 2901 implementation of a CPU may be cleaner, because registers and multiplexers are already built into the chip. The only external register you'll need is for latching the first part of the instruction.

Digital Design Lab Manual

You need to worry about <u>when to pulse the 2901 clock</u>; it can't be active on every cycle; perhaps what's called ACC on the 181 timing diagram can be 2901 clock. But that's not quite safe enough; all the time 2901 clock is low the RAM is liable to be written into; you may want a 1−shot with $\overline{Q}$ output between the "ACC" waveform and the 2901 clock proper. [in fact, ask yourself what comes out of the A and B RAM ports when CLK is low...]

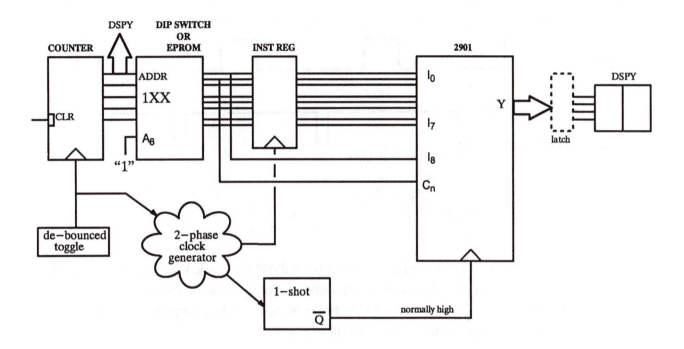

Study the following timing diagram, adapted from the 181 waveforms on the previous page. The bottom waveform for the 2901 clock will have a LOW phase and a rising edge cleanly <u>after</u> the time the 2nd byte has been exposed to the 2901 by the odd phase of the counter LSB. During the odd phase the Y−bus may change on the display.

To correct for odd−phase mistakes, put a latch on the Y−bus, and latch the answer <u>before</u> Q register changes.

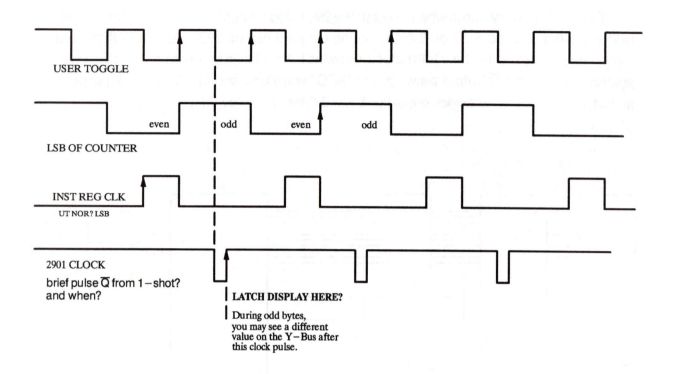

USER TOGGLE

LSB OF COUNTER

even   odd   even   odd

INST REG CLK

UT NOR? LSB

2901 CLOCK

brief pulse $\overline{Q}$ from 1–shot?
and when?

LATCH DISPLAY HERE?

During odd bytes,
you may see a different
value on the Y–Bus after
this clock pulse.

The important line in the timing diagram above is the 2901 clock. What's shown may be too sketchy. You may need to take more care with the timing between the display latch and the 2901. Perhaps the display should be latched before the rising edge of the 2901 clock. Maybe each needs a separate 1–shot. Think about it.

Since the register you select as accumulator is hidden inside the 2901, you *may* need to insert a "NoOp" instruction after other instructions where the accumulator value doesn't remain with the Y outputs. The NoOp brings Q out to Y, without changing any registers. In fact, there are several NoOps in the 2901 code in your EPROM. In the EPROM code suppled for the 2901, there's only one test with NOPs––you have to "interpret" the **Y–bus** output.

The jump problem again. The counter LOAD or CLEAR pin needs to be controlled by the instruction and maybe 2901 status, in order to execute conditional jumps. As with the 181, we have no built−in jump instruction, and must select un−used code to represent JUMP's. Look at the 2901 function table and notice that we don't use the XOR function. (The XNOR is used for the INVERT instruction). If we XOR the accumulator (Q) with data bits 0000, we'll generate a zero output and the F=zero pin will go high. Use this arrangement for the JUMP IF ZERO instruction in the 2901. See next diagram for a way to detect and use the XOR instruction.

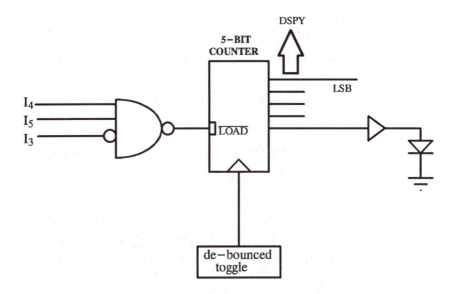

Design in "architecture." Now you can start to see why they call it computer "architecture." Quite a few seemingly equivalent options are available, and one must be selected...Should a door be here or there? One story or two? post−modern or Italian renaissance?

Lab FPGA

A CHALLENGING LAB! CURRENTLY NOT SUPPORTED BY JD. PREFER PAL LAB NOW.

FPGA   Field–programmable gate array multiplier

Design with XACT editLCA software a 4-bit x 4-bit positive number multiplier to be implemented on a Xilinx 3042 field-programmable gate array chip. Have the 8 bits of input be set on DIP switch wired in to the 64 pin wire wrap socket on the BUXUSP board, which houses the 3042. Let the answer appear on 7-segment display chips on the BUXUSP board.

For no FTQ, extend your design to handle 4-bit 2's complement inputs and present 8-bit 2's complement answers.

The BUXUSP board was designed by Bill Patterson at Brown University in 1992. He has written two sets of notes which Lab 12 fans will find of interest: "BUXUSP: The Brown University–Xilinx Universal Small–scale Prototyping Board," and "Hints for using WORK-VIEW and XACT software for Xilinx FPGA design, Part I." The last circuit diagram in the BUXUSP handout shows the pinout for the user socket on the right. On the actual BUXUSP a 60–pin wire–wrap socket is connected by ribbon cable J3 to a breadboard. It is on this breadboard that your DIP switch can make contact with the 3042 input pads.

Setting up BUXUSP.
You need black XILINX security block to plug in series to one of the parallel ports.

You can enter your design connections directly on a computer–graphic version of the 3042 using the editLCA option from the XACT menu. For details, see below.
[Another more abstract way to design the multiplier is to start with the schematic capture software WORKVIEW we have from ViewLogic. After your schematic is properly drawn and labeled, open the XDE Manager and use XMAKE to translate the WORKVIEW schematic into a useable XACT design file. See Patterson handout "Hints..." mentioned above.]

If you use editLCA for changing connections on your schematic specify EXPERT mode before you enter editLCA. Only in EXPERT mode can new connections be established. When you're ready, turn power on for BUXUSP; you should see F on the 7–segment display, and 2 LED bars on. Press RESET on the card at some point before Downloading.

Tutorials. We have available a 50–minute video tape from Xilinx, "The Programmable Gate Array," which you can check out or watch in the lab. Installed on each 386 machine is a

Tutorial directory which has a tutorial for WORKVIEW and for XACT. The written notes for "Day 3" of the Xilinx Programmable Gate Array Training Course book have extensive view-graphs on `editLCA`. A TA or JD will be available for lessons in the use of the software if the tutorials don't provide enough information.

User Guide and Tutorials, Xilinx Corp., 1991. "Using Viewdraw for LCA designs," page 249 ff.

To get to the editLCA program:

1. after machine boots up type `logon`, which executes a batch file;

2. you'll see a red screen; type `9` to exit;

3. type `xilinx` at the DOS prompt; when it asks about WORKVIEW just reply "yes."

4. In a few seconds you'll be in the XACT *Design Manager*.

Under the **PlaceRoute** menu (third from left) select XACT, then hit `done;`

5. After a few seconds you'll be in the XACT *Design Editor*.

6. Click on the part listing and select the 3042PC part, since that's the part on BUXUSP.

7. You might as well go to the C\XACT\DESIGNS\JD directory.

8. Pull down the left−most menu "Program" menu and select the top item *editLCA*. You'll either create a new file or edit an existing one. After a few seconds the screen will fill with a close−up of the FPGA.

[9. To leave editLCA type `exit` in the CMD window at the bottom]

10. If you hold the left mouse button down, you can scan the entire FPGA chip by scooting the mouse around. See in the data book exactly what's in each CLB and I/O block.

11. See below for how to edit and wire up logic and I/O blocks.

STEPS IN GENERATING A PROTOTYPE WITH THE editLCA program for BUXUSP:

1. make sure 3042 chip is selected

2. be in "expert" mode, for editing

3. go to the C\XACT\DESIGNS\JD directory before creating a new file

4. Edit logic blocks and I/O blocks. Lab 12 is a combinatorial design so you don't have to worry about clock signals. In a CLB click on F to type in a combinatorial expression.

5. Click on the BLK menu and select **editBlk**.

6. logic symbols for **editBlk**:

~	NOT
*	AND
+	OR
@	EXOR

Watch the K−map appear after you define F or G!

Click on X to be output F.

to exit use **EndBlk**

7. For I/O blocks, click on output to be O if you want an output pad.

8. Wire pins from the NET menu. Use **AddNet** from the NET menu. You can use to mouse to point at pins in a net list. Use **DelNet** to remove nets.

9. Be sure to SAVE on the command line at the bottom when you leave the diagram.

10. Spread out your design so you don't get to a point where it's not possilbe to route from one point to another.

11. SAVE your design frequently!

When you're finished with editLCA **exit** and go back up to the XACT *Design Manager*. Go to the directory where your file.lca is.

Under the VERIFY menu select MAKEBITS and click on DONE.

MAKEBITS will generate a file.bit.

Under the UTILITIES menu go out to DOS.

Now make sure the power cable is hooked up to BUXUSP and the power is on and the board is reset. Make sure the Xilinx serial cable is connected.

Under DOS hit DIR and see your file.bit. type >xdown file.bit and hit return.

You should see the second LED from the left come on and the screen say, "Done signal has gone high." Even if the DONE light doesn't come on, your file may have been successfully transmitted. When the 3042 is configured with your design you can test it with the DIP switch connections on the 60-pin socket protoboard. Run wires from the DIP switch to the input pads, and from the output pads to the 7-segment control pads (2, 4, 6, etc).

The J3 connector terminates on breadboard with all the even pins on one side and all the odd pins on the other side. The side on which the ribbon cable goes in is the EVEN side of the connector socket! Don't forget to take account of the LS241 enable pin (18 on the cable)!

_____ _____

Field-programmable gate arrays (FPGAs) are many-pinned IC chips. See examples of FPGA chips in the lab. A FPGA contains arrays of cells; each cell is a logic block with, for example, multiplexers and flip flops. Other components are I/O blocks. The designer uses software to configure each cell or block, and lay out connections between the cells to suit his or her specific purpose. You should look through the Xilinx *Programmable Gate Array Data Book* to see what combinatorial and flip flop loigc is in a Xilinx cell, and how the rows and columns of connectors can be used to route signals from one cell to another. Study also the specialized input-output cells.

Lab F

F   Electronic Synapse

INTRODUCTION A real synapse is a connection between one nerve cell's output axon and another nerve cell's input dendrite. There are about 10^{12} neurons and 10^{15} synapses in a human brain.

Our electronic synapse attempts to emulate some properties of modifiable synapses. In a neural networks course you'll learn about the error correction update rule for synaptic modification of a weight W,

$$\Delta W_{ij} = \eta \cdot \delta_i \cdot x_j$$

$$W_{ij-new} = W_{ij-old} + \Delta W_{ij}$$

Where η is the learning rate $\ll 1$, δ_i is the error correction term for unit i and x_j is the input to weight W_{ij}.

In this lab you'll create an electronic, digital−analog version, of this operation.

REQUIREMENTS: Build a circuit which will solve *approximately* the differential equation system below, which represents associative learning:

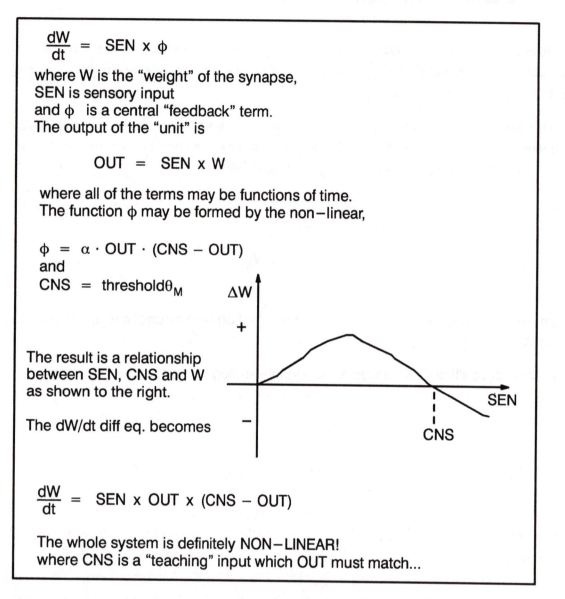

$$\frac{dW}{dt} = \text{SEN} \times \phi$$

where W is the "weight" of the synapse,
SEN is sensory input
and ϕ is a central "feedback" term.
The output of the "unit" is

$$\text{OUT} = \text{SEN} \times W$$

where all of the terms may be functions of time.
The function ϕ may be formed by the non−linear,

$$\phi = \alpha \cdot \text{OUT} \cdot (\text{CNS} - \text{OUT})$$
and
$$\text{CNS} = \text{threshold}\theta_M$$

The result is a relationship between SEN, CNS and W as shown to the right.

The dW/dt diff eq. becomes

$$\frac{dW}{dt} = \text{SEN} \times \text{OUT} \times (\text{CNS} - \text{OUT})$$

The whole system is definitely NON−LINEAR!
where CNS is a "teaching" input which OUT must match...

We restrict SEN and Φ to positive numbers, in fact to pulse trains where the pulse *rate* equals SEN or ϕ, the same way pulses travel on nerve cell axons.

With regard to synaptic modification, what's going on here?

If dW/dt were simply equal to SEN x OUT, then the weight could only increase. Our system allows the weight to *increase, decrease, or fluctuate around a stable value*. The ability to decrease synaptic weight gives our system important learning properties.

If SEN = 0 or CNS = 0, no weight modification can take place. If CNS = SEN then the system has found a stable value for weight. For one SEN input, the system "learns" to make SEN about

Digital Design Lab Manual

equal to CNS by adjusting W. The diagram below illustrates how the modifiable synapse can be described in block diagram form.

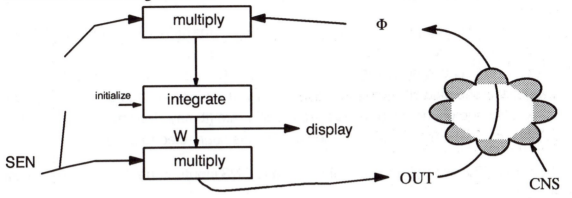

The top "multiplier" will be replaced with an AND gate which can respond to **pulses** on the peripheral and central input paths.

The integrator will be an 8–bit counter, connected to your display chip. Count direction will form the F function from the CNS pulse train.

The bottom multiplier will be your DAC, with variable ref.

Other reading:

Simon Haykin, <u>Fundamentals of Neural Networks</u>, MacMillian (1994).

How to demonstrate your circuit works:

Display the output of the counter on 2 digits of the 7433. Be able to initialize your counter to 35_{16}; you don't need a DIP switch for initialization...the data lines can be hard–wired to 35_{16}. The initial count is the status of the synapse at "birth."

<u>The loading of 35 must be automatic</u>...use only your toggle switch to "begin labor."

Monitor the output of the DAC op amp with your voltmeter.

To begin with don't connect the DAC op amp output to the 555 pin 5.

Transmit pulses onto the SEN & CNS inputs; have the pulse rates ≈ to each other. Send a higher frequency pulse train onto SEN and we'll watch the counter decrease its 8–bit output until it reaches 00, at which point it will **stop**, and not roll over to FF_{16}.* When the count is near 00 the voltmeter should read near a minimum for DAC output. Decrease the sensory pulse rate (654 can be connected to a variable voltage potentiometer) until it is less than the CNS rate; the count direction should reverse and the counter should count up until it reaches FF_{16}, at which point it will **stop**, and not roll over to 00. The DAC op amp output should now be near a maximum, given its reference.

---

* You probably designed something like this to stop rollover for lab 8, the DA lab. It may matter whether you use $\overline{CET}$ or $\overline{CEP}$ to send the inverted $\overline{RCO}$ back to. Note that $\overline{RCO}$ depends on count direction.

If CNS input is <u>grounded</u> (CNS rate = 0) then counting should freeze.
That's all you need for a basic check off of lab F!

Now connect the output of the DAC op amp to pin 5 of the 555 and start over at 35. What happens? Is the "dynamic range" of the synapse extended?
What effect does changing voltage on pin 5 your 555 have on output of the 555?
What does the 555 data sheet say happens when you vary the voltage on pin 5? Usually increasing voltage on the pin 5 **decreases** the 555 rate (it may also change duty cycle). Does this explain the result you see when the DAC is connected to pin 5?

Possible FTQ: what will happen if the SEN and CNS inputs to the direction control are reversed?

Note: Don't disassemble your circuit when you finish; we'll save all the completed lab F's and at the end of the semester build them into a little brain. At least we'll see if a device can be made which exhibits associative learning. As you can infer from the diagram on the previous page, each synapse per unit will receive a different SEN input, and each will receive the <u>same</u> CNS feedback.

Discussion

The integrator will be an 8-bit counter (use both the 169 & 2569). The integrator's "clock" input will come from an AND gate output. The AND gate will be used as a <u>coincidence detector</u>, switching to high output when both SEN and CNS are simultaneously high. Actually, you might find that a NAND gate will work just as well as an AND. An OR gate would not be appropriate as a coincidence detector.

Up/Down on the counter will be determined by whether CNS is pulsing more rapidly than SEN; Arrange that the <u>maximum rate</u> of the 654 can be greater than the 555 CNS rate. A good choice for rates is around 100 Hz. With regard to the digital integrator, its count must stop if FF_{16} is reached **and** the count direction is up; the count must also stop if 00 is reached **and** the direction is down. Normally a digital counter will roll over at FF and 00...you don't want your counter to roll over. Study the active-low ripple carry out's of your counters to see how to realize this feature. Note that you want to stop at FF and 00, **not** F0 and 0F, so you may need to deal with both RCO's in a circuit which stops counting. Furthermore, you want counting to start again if count directions changes. How is RCO related to count direction? You may need to study carefully the differences between parallel and trickle enables on your counters; one of these enables will be appropriate for stopping at FF and 00_{16}, the other won't. See the *Digital Design from Zero to One* chpt. 6 on counters.

The integrator will form the digital input to your DAC, as it did in Lab 8. The DAC's reference will come from a pulse rate "tachometer" circuit connected to the sensory input.

This schematic provides a general solution to Lab F; other details follow.

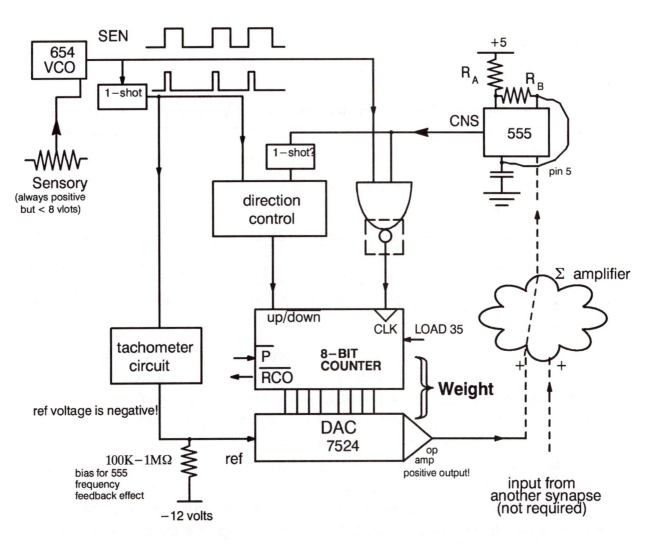

More Discussion. You need one op amp to complete the DAC, and the other op amp for the tachometer circuit; you have 2 op amps in your one LF 353. Your 555 can be used to generate CNS pulses; the 555 can do double duty and also provide switching for your 2–digit display; we don't care if your display flickers unevenly.

Let's look at the requirements of **direction control**. Direction control needs to enforce the following rule: *If SEN rate is greater than CNS rate, count down, if SEN rate is less than CNS rate, count up.* In order to avoid potential timing problems we can use the following (conservative) shift register idea:

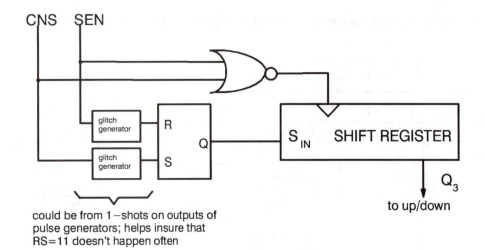

could be from 1−shots on outputs of pulse generators; helps insure that RS=11 doesn't happen often

If there are more SEN than CNS pulses/sec, then the shift register will fill with 0's, the up/down pin will see 0, and digital integrator will count down. Vice versa for SEN > CNS rate. The longer the shift register, the more sluggish the system. To avoid SR = 11 on the set−reset flip flop, you will need to place "pulse shrinkers" on the inputs; see § 5 on edge−triggered flips for information.

We show Q_3 as an example. Notice that whenever a coincidence occurs, R and S will be high simultaneously, and what goes from Q to S_{IN} will depend on the particular design you use for the SR flip flop. However, since data is clocked in only on the falling edge of SEN ∨ CNS, the shift register will almost never have to deal with uncertain input.
Another example of an asynchronous sequential circuit.

The rule for weight change

If two synapses feed into the same summation amplifier, and that summation amplifier helps generate the feedback learning signal, then the weight will increase if SEN is less than CNS, and decrease if SEN is greater than CNS. In other words, the synaptic weight change is helping SEN learn what CNS is.
The output of the "neuron" is seeking the CNS level.

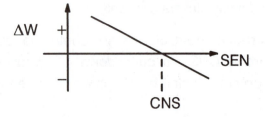

If increasing DAC output (representing the cell output) causes CNS to **decrease**, then for a fixed SEN input SEN and CNS should become equal at some point. See Bienenstock, Cooper & Munro, "Theory for the development of neuron selectivity: Orientation specificity and binocular interaction in visual cortex," *J. Neurosci 2*: 32−48 (1982).

Here's a suggestion for use of the 654 as a positive voltage input oscillator:

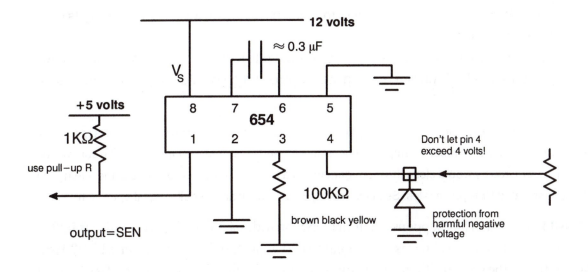

Read the 654 data sheet for more details and precautions. If you use the positive voltage configuration, don't place a negative voltage on pin 4, or the chip will become vaporware! In fact, try to stay in the range 0 to 5 volts, since a positive voltage near the +12 power level isn't good for the chip either. You may want to consider putting a 1–shot on the output of the 654, to shorten the duration of the pulses forming SEN input; by this means the tachometer circuit will change output values more than if it's always looking at a 50% duty cycle pulse train.

Now consider the **tachometer circuit**, which can also be described as a *leaky integrator*.

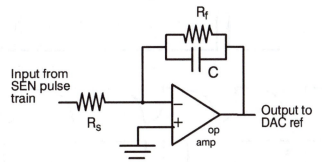

The input is either 0 or a positive voltage. This circuit turns a pulse train input into an average value output. Due to the negative gain of the op amp, the output = ref will be negative, but that's OK, it'll be inverted again on the other side of the DAC, providing a positive output to send to the 555 pin 5.

The parallel RC combination in the amplifier feedback path acts as a low–pass filter; in particular, the capacitor acts as an integrator, while the resistor is the "leak". Try 100KΩ and 0.3μF for the R_f resistor & capacitor values of the leaky integrator; these values should be compatible with the pulse rate of the VCO, but you may have to fiddle around with them. See the timing diagram below. The source resistor R_S should be a value which will give a low frequency gain near -1. If the output of the tach circuit is too low, try increasing its gain by varying resistors R_f or R_s.

You might want to connect a 1MΩ resistor from -12 volts to the summation pin of the DAC op amp, to insure the DAC output never goes to zero, which would cause the 555 to shut down.

The tachometer + DAC circuit could be replaced by an all–digital circuit. The DAC output is really only useful for connection to a summation amplifier which sees other DAC signals as inputs too. The summation amplifier + other circuitry would close the loop, generating a CNS pulse train whose rate is the average of the all the associated SEN pulse rates. See *Optional Topic* below for another all–digital approach.

Possible FTQ's: What happens when the CNS provides a 50% duty cycle pulse train? Is the 1–shot next to the 654 necessary? What would happen if CNS were always high? How can you initialize the system if there are no pulses on the SEN line? What happens if we pull out an RCO pin? How will reducing the size of the 1–shot capacitor affect the counting rate?

Below we show a partial timing diagram for **counting up**, with CNS < SEN rate.

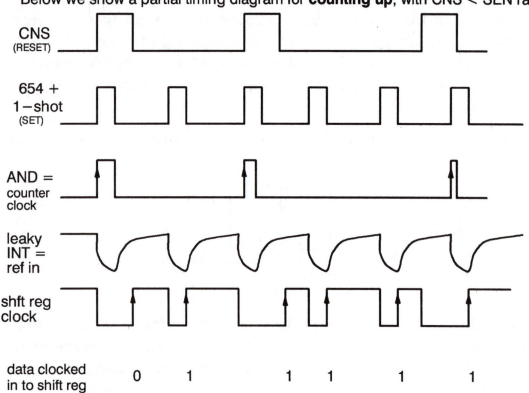

up/down will be mostly high, but we can't show exactly what Q_3 will be because we haven't specified the initial condition of the shift register.

Notice that the counter clock signals are separated in time from the shift register clock signals; there should be no time when both occur simultaneously...does this mean we can do without the shift register and let up/down be determined with SR flip flop output? You may want to draw out another timing diagram with RCO's to solve the stopping problem.

Optional Topic: **Digital replacement for DAC**. We can make a digital replacement for the DAC by noting that what we really want to do, in the pulse–dependent electronic synapse, is modify the pulse rate of SEN, and send the modified rate into an overall rate averager with other associated pulse trains. (Eventually all the averaged pulses will help generate a CNS feedback.) In the same way that an 8–bit multiplying DAC gives a fraction $W/256$ of its reference, where W = weight and $0 \leq W \leq 255$, we would like our fractional pulse transmitter to pass $W/256$ pulses out of every 256 pulses on SEN. We call the circuit below a "pulse killer" because its effect is to eliminate a fraction of SEN pulses, based on synaptic weight W.

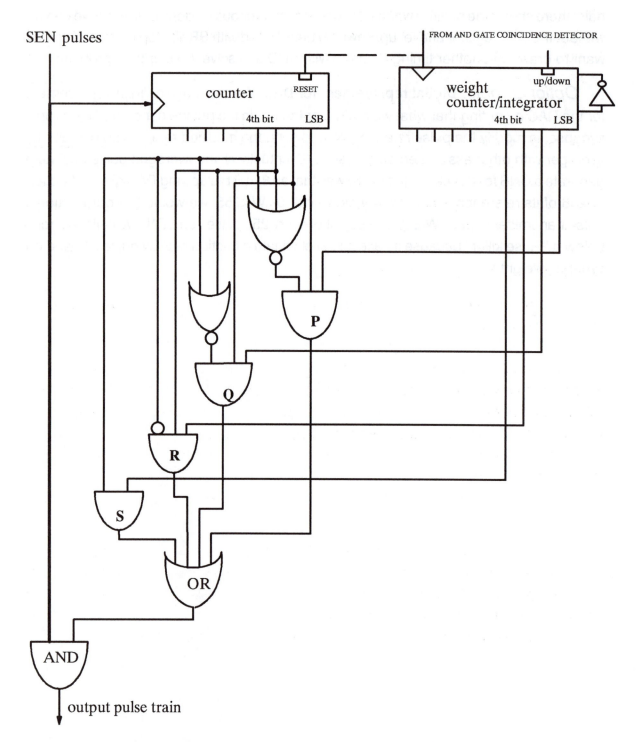

The maximum rate that will pass (for 8 bits = 1111 1111) is 255/256 of SEN. We show the idea, using only the first four bits of weight output combined with a 4−bit counter.

Explanation of the pulse killer. If the bottom AND gate sees a 1 from the OR gate feeding it, then all the SEN pulses will pass through. But look what happens if the weight is 1000:

Only AND–S will be active and only half of the SEN pulses will be enabled to pass through the bottom AND gate. Now consider weight = 0001. Only AND–P can be active, and it will be active only when the left counter output = 0001, that is, 1/16 of the time. The three input NOR gate feeding AND–P will be 1 <u>only</u> when its (non–LSB) inputs are 000. Various other combinations of weight values will result in W/16 of the SEN pulses passing through the bottom AND gate. In particular, if W = 0000, then **no** pulses pass through the bottom AND. What happens when the weight changes, due to detection of a SEN/CNS coincidence? We show one possibility: the left counter is reset and starts over at 0000. Presumably SEN pulses come into the system at a rate much greater that the weight changes. The worst case will be when CNS rate > SEN rate, so that the weight is changing at rate comparable to SEN; in this case the reset feature may not be necessary for reasonable operation of the circuit.Can you think of a way to kill SEN pulses on an 8–bit system without scaling the above idea up to 7 input NOR & 8–input OR gates?

The main advantage of the all digital DAC: the whole synapse circuit now becomes all digital, and we don't need the tachometer circuit shown before. An all–digital circuit may be easier to lay out as an integrated circuit.

Another possible annoyance: The direct connection of SEN to the output AND gate has less delay than the signal from the OR gate which can disable the output AND. What problems could this cause in timing? Will too many pulses sneak through? How often does the output of the OR change, compared to the SEN pulse train?

Another point we haven't worried about too much for the circuitry described: What should the duty cycle of the SEN and CNS pulse trains be? In general, the briefer the pulse, the more like a multiplier will be the action of the coincidence detector, but the greater the pulse rate attenuation.

The normalization problem. We haven't addressed it, but suppose a neural network had to have its synaptic weights add up to a constant; if one went way up, the others would all have to go down a little. We could attack this with a "sleep cycle." During sleep all inputs become 1; if the output of a cell is greater than 1, then a count down signal is sent to all weight counters, until the cell output = 1 (this would be a negative feedback system).

10   Digital Filter, High Pass

Design and build a high-pass digital filter.
Convert an analog sine wave signal (obtained from a Tektronix function generator module) to 7-bit digital resolution using the AD7576 chip. Clock the 7576 at a rate which produces one conversion every msec. Subtract the previous conversion from the current one, then D/A convert the difference and display the result on an oscilloscope. Show that for low sine wave frequencies the D/A output is about zero, and for frequencies around 100 Hz a "differentiated" sine wave appears. Have a second mode of operation in which the A/D code is passed without subtraction to the D/A converter, and the original plus converted waveforms displayed for comparison on the oscilloscope. Demonstrate aliasing for input frequencies greater than 500 Hz.

Discussion.
If you're unfamiliar with the operation of an oscilloscope (use CHOP for two simultaneous signals) consult a TA or the professor; likewise, consult for unfamiliarity with the sine wave generator.

The filter is "high pass" because for low frequencies (low rates of change of input, compared to the A/D converter rate) the output is nearly zero. Nearly equal numbers are subtracted every msec, and their difference is almost zero. If the ALU were to add instead of subtract, you would have a low−pass filter.

Use the **AD 7576**, 8−bit A/D converter. You won't have to do lab 9 over! Study the 7576 data sheet, noting limits on the voltages to be applied. Included with the 7576 data sheets are a couple of pages from *Analog−Digital Conversion Handbook* (Prentice−Hall, 1986), which discuss 7576 timing and mode.
Notice that the 7576 uses a natural binary code to represent analog values. The data sheets don't spell out exactly what the control signals do for starting conversion or latching output. We provide additional information below.
The 7576 has three "logic" inputs ($\overline{CS}$, $\overline{RD}$, MODE) and one logic−status output ($\overline{BUSY}$). $\overline{BUSY}$ is active−low during the conversion. The duration of $\overline{BUSY}$, compared to the 1 msec period on the 555, is rather brief!
A conversion is started when any one of the logic inputs goes from HI to LO. Internally, a flip

flop is SET by the action, and it's reset by the end−of−conversion.

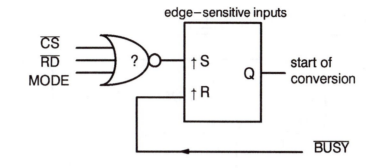

If MODE is LO and $\overline{RD}$ is HI, then the 7576 converts continually; we don't want this mode because we want to limit the time between conversion to 1 msec. Let MODE be tied HI. Let $\overline{RD}$ receive the 555 pulses, and regulate the start of conversion.

When is valid digital data latched at the output? When $\overline{RD}$ goes from HI to LO the conversion completed *during the previous $\overline{BUSY}$ pulse* is latched in the 7576 output.

TIMING DIAGRAM FOR 7576 DATA LATCH SHOWN BELOW.

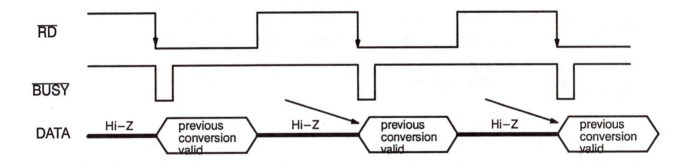

The 3−state output of 7576 is enabled when $\overline{CS}$ & $\overline{RD}$ are LO simultaneously.
The 7576 can be hooked up like this—

Digital Design Lab Manual

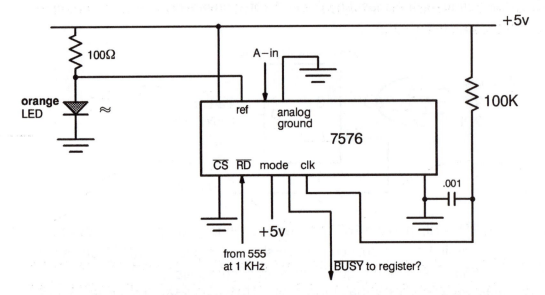

Let the 7576 run on its internal clock, using the 100K resistor from "clock" pin 5 to V_{DD} (5v), and a small capacitor from pin 5 to ground. As long as the internal clock is running much faster than the 555, the 7576 will finish a conversion in much less than 1 msec, *the time between conversions*. In the case shown, a conversion will be over in about 20 *microsec-*onds (Check the duration of $\overline{BUSY}$ LO on the oscilloscope, if you like). Because the conversion time is so fast, the lack of sample−and−hold on the input may not be a big problem. For "reference" voltage we don't have to be picky. Let the forward voltage drop (about 2v) of a low impedance <u>orange</u> LED do the job. The size of "ref" affects the maximum peak−to−peak amplitude of the input waveform which can be converted.

If the 7576 ADC output is passed through to the 7524 DAC, the output will look something like this for a 50Hz sine wave input.

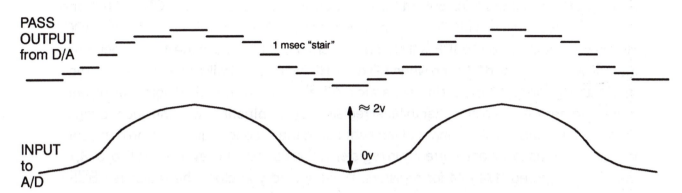

PASS
OUTPUT
from D/A

1 msec "stair"

$\approx$ 2v

0v

INPUT
to
A/D

Test that your 7576 works by sending in an analog signal of 0−2 volt size from your potentiometer. You should be able to monitor changing D0−D7 with your logic probe (or hex display); it will work like an 7−8−bit version of Lab 9. After you're sure it's acquiring data, hook the 7576 up to a sine wave of frequency < 500 Hz. Use the OFFSET and AMPLITUDE controls to insure the input sine wave stays between limits of 0−2 v.

In the PASS mode you can observe aliasing by turning up the frequency. What formula predicts the alias frequency for an input greater than the sampling frequency? Try to count how many levels of quantization can you see on the oscilloscope, for the sine wave presented as input?

The most conservative way to obtain two digital numbers for subtraction is pass the ADC output through two registers in series (pipeline, taped delay line).

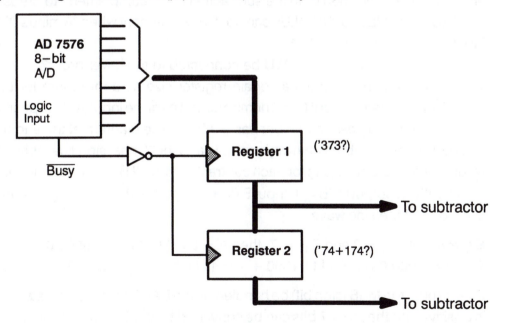

AD 7576
8−bit
A/D

Logic
Input

$\overline{\text{Busy}}$

Register 1   ('373?)

To subtractor

Register 2   ('74+174?)

To subtractor

Make sure that register 2 captures data <u>before</u> register 1 changes! This circuit does have extra delay which may be a handicap in a system which must run at top speed.

Latching the previous ADC output for subtraction. If you ground both $\overline{CS}$ and $\overline{RD}$, and send the 1KHz clock into MODE, you might get away with just one register after the ADC. HI−to−LO transition on MODE will start a conversion. Otherwise, if the 1KHz clock goes into $\overline{RD}$ with MODE tied HI, then when $\overline{RD}$ goes HI, 7576 output will become Hi−Z, so you must latch the first ADC output in a separate register 1, as shown in the diagram at the end. Place another 7−bit register after the first register (form a **pipeline**) with the second register output headed to the "B" input of the subtractor; the second register will hold the conversion previous to the one currently in register 1. You can use the level−sensitive '373, or the edge triggered '174+74 for registers. What should you clock the registers? $\overline{BUSY}$ (end−of−conversion) pulse, or the 555, or some 1−shot?
When should the latching occur?

Think of a way to CLEAR the second register so that it can present all 0's to the subtractor. (Too bad the '382 doesn't have a "PASS" function, or you could control subtract vs pass with function−select on the ALUs.) When in the CLEAR mode, the present digital code will be passed from the 7576 through the 7524, with no subtraction of prior code. During CLEAR mode, as you increase the sine wave frequency above 500 Hz, you'll observe aliasing of high frequencies disguised as lower frequencies.

Subtraction. You need to think carefully about how to do the subtraction of current−previous (A−B in the diagram at the end), and how to send the resulting difference to the DAC. "A" is the present 7576 digital output, and "B" is the previous output. Read text §1 on codes and arithmetic. You should do the subtraction in 2's complement, to prepare the code for the DAC. The '382 and '181 ALUs can do 2's complement when "A minus B" is the selected function and carry$_{in}$ is set to 1.
How should the higher order ALU be connected to the lower order?
Two's complement assumes a certain register size as a maximum for the numbers involved. In our case we want 8−bit numbers, and all of the inputs will be positive numbers. *In 2's complement a positive number has a 0 MSB*. The diagram at the end of this write−up shows the MSBs for both pathways set to 0, and the 7 most significant bits of the 7576 digital output as the other 7 bits for each subtractor input. If B > A, then a negative number will result, with an output MSB = 1. Input B (from the register) will be greater than A on the negative slope of the sine wave.

Example: If $A_{10} = 3$ and $B_{10} = 7$, then A = 0000 0011, B = 0000 0111, and
A − B = 0000 0011 + 1111 1000 + 1 = 1111 1100 = -4_{10} in 2's complement.

How should the MSB (sign bit) be handled by the DAC? If the sign bit is **zero**, the difference is positive and the lower 7 bits can be converted by the DAC directly to an analog voltage.

If the sign bit is **one**, then the difference is negative. The whole 8−bit number is in 2's complement form. The sign bit must now exert a "negative" influence on the analog output. Pass the MSB through a negative gain op amp and sum that on the DAC op amp inverting input pin. The DAC terminates in a <u>negative</u> gain op amp. Positive sine wave inputs will therefore result in negative DAC output voltages.

In 2's complement the smallest negative number is

1111 1111 = -1_{10}. So...arrange that 0111 1111 into the DAC almost cancels the effect of 1000 0000 through the MSB op amp.

The largest negative number in 2's comp is 1000 0000. Arrange that MSB=1 exerts the maximum "negative" influence in the 80_{16} case.

And when the input is 0111 1111 arrange that the largest positive voltage occurs.

You may have to adjust the gain resistors of the MSB op amp, and you may have to adjust the R_S resistor from the MSB op amp to the inverting op amp connected to the DAC.

The 7524 data sheet shows how to hook up the 7524 for offset binary negative numbers and a sort of 4 quadrant multiplier. Is offset binary good enough? Maybe not.

So consider what would happen if the MSB is driven by −5v instead of +5 volts. Do we have a 2's complement DAC? The diagram below shows what to do if the DAC is made of direct resistor connections. Unfortunately, the 7524 throws switches from ground to ref rail, so something different is needed. See the summation unit on the main circuit diagram, at the bottom right. Why can we send the DAC output and the 2's comp directly into a summation amplifier? (You may need to adjust gain of MSB compared to DAC's negative output...)

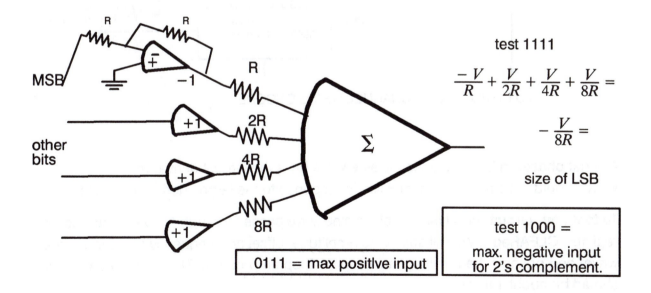

test 1111

$$\frac{-V}{R} + \frac{V}{2R} + \frac{V}{4R} + \frac{V}{8R} =$$

$$-\frac{V}{8R} =$$

size of LSB

0111 = max positive input

test 1000 =

max. negative input for 2's complement.

Digital Design Lab Manual

Schematic suggestion. See previous diagram for 7576 details.

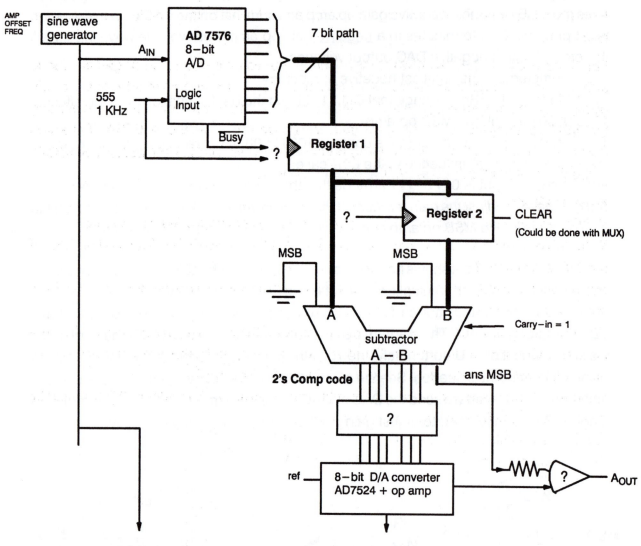

TO DISPLAY ON 2–CHANNEL OSCILLOSCOPE

At what phases in its cycle does the sine wave have the largest derivative?
What should the circuit output look like in response to the large–derivative phase?

To test your circuit, we'll first look at the sine wave passed through A–D–A (subtraction register "CLEARed"). We will adjust the amplitude, offset and frequency of the input sine wave, and observe the resulting staircase DAC op amp output. The width of each stair should be about 1 msec.
How many steps of output magnitude can you resolve? 2^7?
By increasing the input frequency above 500 Hz, we'll see aliasing at the output.

Digital Design Lab Manual

Next the subtractor will be put into action and the high−pass feature of the digital filter can be demonstrated. (Is the DAC staircase still 1msec in width?)
How does frequency of input affect subtractor output? Is the output nearly zero for low frequency?

For some phases of the sine wave input, the output voltage should be **negative**, due to subtraction of a larger number from a smaller one. (Negative numbers may be positive voltages, because of negative gain in the DAC op amp.) Can you see any subtraction aliasing for high frequency input? Switch back and forth between CLEAR and SUBTRACT at a high frequency, and see if the alias frequency is the same. At just the right frequency, you should see a 90° phase shift from input to subtracted output.

Possible FTQ's:
Would sample−and−hold improve the performance of the circuit? Why or why not?
What will output look like if the 6−bit 74174 is used as the "previous" register, and the LSB of input B is grounded?
How should the design be changed if you want to subtract the conversion **two** cycles ago from the current conversion?
What will happen to the output waveform frequency if the input frequency exceeds the sampling rate (500 Hz) of the 1000 Hz "mode" clock? What formula allows you to calculate the alias frequency, given the sampling rate and the input frequency?
What waveform changes will occur if the subtractor is turned into an adder? What should be done with the MSB in the case of the adder?
Is there any possibility for arithmetic OVERFLOW?
What happens to the 7576 if $\overline{CS}$ is connected to HI?

Aliasing of frequencies above Nyquist rate

Any *periodic* waveform can be expressed by the Fourier series as a summation of sine and cosine functions. If x(t) is such a waveform, then

$$x(t) = a_0 + 2 \sum_{n=1}^{N} a_n \cos(n\omega_0 t) + 2 \sum_{n=1}^{N} b_n \sin(n\omega_0 t)$$

Where $N \cdot \omega_0$ is the maximum frequency in waveform x(t).

What is ω_0? It is the lowest frequency (other than DC) in x(t). $\omega_0 = 2\pi f_0$ & $f_0 = 1/T_0$, where T_0 is the period of x(t).

How many unknowns must be solved for to describe x(t) completely?

There are N a_n's + N b_n's + a_0. A total of 2N+1.

In how short of an interval do we need to sample 2N+1 times?

We must sample in T_0 time, or the waveform will "repeat."

The sampling frequency f_s then is computed by $f_s = \dfrac{T_0}{2N + 1}$

Expressed in terms of T_0, the maximum frequency in the waveform is

$$f_{max} = \frac{N \cdot \omega_0}{2} pi = \frac{N \cdot 2\pi}{2\pi \cdot T_0} = \frac{N}{T_0}$$

Therefore the waveform must be sampled at a rate at least twice as great as the maximum frequency in the waveform.

You don't really have to sample a periodic waveform; the 2N+1 samples you take in less than T_0 time can be used to construct a waveform that can be (mathematically) repeated. In other words, we're not going to sample a waveform forever...

Now suppose we don't sample fast enough, or the maximum frequency in the waveform increases without our increasing our sampling rate. What happens?

The input frequencies above f_s will appear in the output disguised as low frequencies (aliasing)

Easiest way to a formula: Try convolution, which is multiplication in frequency domain

$\omega_a = 2\pi f$

$f_a = f_{in} \bmod f_s$

For f_s = 500 Hz, 560 Hz will appear as 60 Hz; 960 Hz will appear as 460 Hz.

Sampling in time. **Suppose we want to A−D convert a sine wave oscillating at 1KHz. It seems likely that if we sample at 10,000 times per second, we could make a good re−construction...at least get the frequency right. But what if we sample at a lower frequency, say 100 times per second...can we still get a reconstruction? Seems doubtful; we'd be sampling only once every ten cycles. Equally bad, what if we sample at 1KHz? We'll get the same answer at every sample, be-**

cause our data will be at the same phase of the wave each time!
Neither of the last two (low) rates is satisfactory. We need to sample at at least 2x the highest
frequency of the input in order to get a faithful frequency reproduction of the signal (2000 times
per sec, for the example). Otherwise we get aliasing—a higher frequency disguising itself as a
lower frequency in the reproduction. Let's take an expanded look at sampling rate. During the
discussion keep in mind there are two frequencies involved − − the frequency of the input signal
and the frequency of the sampling.

(The following analysis is after
Chuck Williams, *Designing Digital Filters, Prentice−Hall* (1986) **chpt 1, pp.'s 13−16.**)

In A/D, there are quantization errors of magnitude (resolution errors)...and errors due to time
sampling.
Errors of magnitude won't concern us here. Furthermore we assume proper sample & hold
takes place on the input. The easy way out is to sample frequently enough to insure that all
waveforms are accounted for. But we pay two prices for this sort of over−engineering: (1) We
may pay extra for A/D circuits which have a fast acquisition time—remember from last § that A/D
conversion always take **time**, the shortest time taken by $$ flash converters (2) We may pay extra for the
memory to hold all those numbers we're acquiring.
The faster a signal is changing, the more rapidly we'll have to sample to "keep up" with it, but
what is a more precise way to say this?

Imagine a sine wave of **one** frequency, ωt, where ω is in **radians**.
Our input, $A_{in}(t) = \sin \omega t$. (What annoyances would we have if ω weren't expressed in radians?).
At regular intervals τ our digital machine samples and acquires (with some N−bit magnitude
resolution) "snapshots" of $A_{in}(t)$. We can save these samples as a **list in memory** of
$A_{con}(k) = \sin \omega k\tau = \sin \omega\tau \cdot k$.
Our problem is, how can we use the list $A_{con}(k)$ to discover what ω was in $A_{in}(t)$?

The factor $\omega\tau$ can be called a "sampling angle"; it has the dimension of radians. The smaller $\omega\tau$,
the more times per sine wave cycle we will sample, and the better will be our eventual re−con-
struction (spectrum analysis). Think about it: if τ is small we'll be sampling often; if ω is small
$A_{in}(t) = \sin \omega t$ won't change quickly. Now suppose we lengthen τ until
$\omega\tau = 2\pi$. Since k is an integer, we will be sampling at $k2\pi$ intervals of $A_{in}(t)$, and getting **the**
same answer every time! ($\sin 2\pi = \sin k2\pi$), an undesirable situation...

What if τ gets longer and $\omega\tau > 2\pi$? We can partition $\omega\tau = \omega_0 + \Omega$,
where $\omega_0 < 2\pi$ and
$\Omega = $ integer x 2π.
Now $A_{con}(k) = \sin \omega\tau \cdot k = \sin (\omega_0 + \Omega) \cdot k = \sin (\omega_0 k + \Omega k) = \sin (\omega_0 k + $ integer x $2\pi)$
But $\sin ($anything $ + $ integer$\cdot 2\pi) = \sin ($anything$)$, so
$A_{con}(k) = \sin \omega_0 k$, and we find that **frequency ω has aliased itself as lower frequency ω_0.**

To say it another way: If our "sampling angle" $\omega\tau$ is greater than 2π, then the the angle ω will look, in the sample−list generated by our τ A/D converter, **identical** to the data produced by a lower frequency ω_0.

Example: (assume sine wave is about 1000 Hz as above...) Imagine joining the circled points—they would look nothing like the original data of the sine wave.

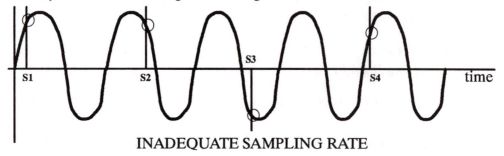

INADEQUATE SAMPLING RATE

By the terminology we've generated, we can say that, if we want **no** aliasing, we'd like $\Omega = 0$, with a residual $\omega\tau < 2\pi$. This relationship means, as a criterion for τ, we'd like $\tau < 2\pi/\omega$. But when we started, we put ω in radians, for the sake of computation. $\omega_{rad} = 2\pi \cdot \omega_{Hz}$. So, if we consider ω in **cycles per sec = Hz,** our criterion for τ is $\tau < 1/\omega$.

Oops. we're off by a factor of 2 from Shannon's sampling theorem result, which says we need to sample **twice per input period (Nyquist rate),** or that our sampling frequency needs to be twice our highest input frequency to avoid aliasing. Our mistake came with the $\omega\tau < 2\pi$ statement; it should really say $\omega\tau < \pi$. Sine and cosine functions, in a sense, duplicate themselves every π radians. Think about it. At any rate, our derivation does give us a reasonable explanation for aliasing.

We've simplified things by considering an input of a pure sine wave of one frequency. Recall that arbitrary waveforms (even non−periodic ones?) can be synthesized from combinations of sine & cosine waves of different frequencies and amplitudes (Fourier series for periodic waveforms; Fourier transform for arbitrary waveforms). If the actual input has other frequencies, then our conversion process can handle them if they're **lower** frequency than ω, but what if they're higher?

What should we do about high input frequencies if our A/D sample rate can't keep up with them? *Filter them out before they get to the A→D circuit.* Filtering requires an analog anti−aliasing low−pass filter—a network of R's and C's. Such a network can filter a large percentage of the high frequency components of the input, but not all of it. We may be left with a small− amplitude high−frequency part of the input signal, which, we will hope, does not contribute much to the A/D list of numbers our sampling will generate.

From the preceding discussion you can appreciated that our understanding of data collected by an A/D converter will be simplified if the time per conversion is always the same (τ, in the case above). Recall that for the counting converter, conversion time depended on how many counts had to be made in the search for an answer, so a counting converter, in the form described in the last §, would not be a good candidate for consistent converter.

11   Asynchronous Shepherd

Woolly sheep are in a barn. If the barn door DB is open and the field door DF is closed, then a sheep will go into the pen. After the barn door is closed, the sheep will be sheared. If a sheared sheep is in the pen and DF opens, while DB is closed, then the sheep will go into the field. A sheep goes into the pen after any DB open–close sequence with field door closed. See diagram.
(Draw in your own sheep; read <u>The Little Prince</u> for help.)

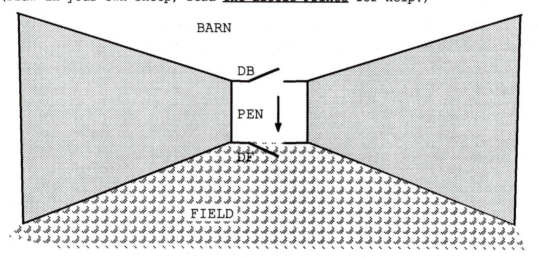

We want a circuit, attached to door-opening detectors, which can signal when a sheep has been sheared and has gone into the field. The output will go HI in the following types of sequence:
(1=door open)

DF	DB	OUT
0	0	0
0	1	0
0	0	0
1	0	0
0	0	1
0	1	0
0	0	0
0	1	0
0	0	0
1	0	0
0	0	1
1	0	0

In general, if the field door is closed while the barn door is open, then the barn door is closed, then the field door is open, the output will come on.

If both doors are open at once, then the system must wait until the barn door is closed before looking again for a sheared-sheep to enter from the field side.

Design and build a circuit which produces a HI output for the door opening and closing sequence given. Have an "LED" light when the sequence has been detected.

NO OSCILLATORS ALLOWED IN THE CIRCUIT. ONLY TWO INPUTS--DB AND DF. NO MORE THAN 5 LATCHES ARE ALLOWED IN THE DESIGN.

If you build the circuit with kit hardware, use two buttons from your keyboard. As you can see from the sequence above, there is no need for debouncing.

You are allowed and encouraged to use LogicWorks or Beige Bag layout and simulation software for lab 11.

Before starting lab 11, read supplemental text Chapter, "Sequential Circuits without Clocks." Since both DB and DF can be HI at the same time, the pulse mode restriction does not necessarily apply. This circuit, like all asynchronous circuits we consider, is governed by the restriction of the fundamental mode--only one input at a time can change, and no subsequent change until after the circuit stabilizes.

Incomplete timing diagram:

Several state transitions from the primitive flow table are not included here.

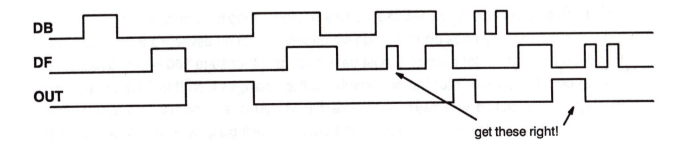

get these right!

Digital Design Lab Manual

Incomplete primitive flow table.

Several arrows are missing. Where should they go?

Each primitive state should have two arrows *leaving*.

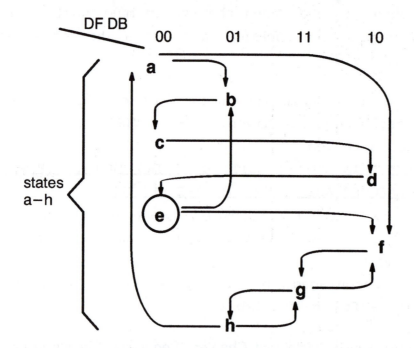

DF DB

Do we have enough states? too many?

Consider pairs of rows from the primitive flow table; label each column for stable state, transient state, or don't–care. Can you merge some of the rows? What about merging f, g & h? With 8 rows (states), you will need <u>at least</u> 3 flip flops for the design.

Suppose you keep all 8 rows. You may want to be careful how you label the states with the flip flop outputs.

For example, if you label
          a – 000
          d – 100
          e – 101
          h – 110

then the transition from d to e will require **two** flip flop changes, and so will the transition from h to a. Since flip flops don't change simultaneously in an asynchronous circuit, the transition from h to a, for example, must pass through either state **100** = d or **010** on the way to **000**. It will be a "race" to see which flip flop changes first. If the system passes through flip flop state d, you may be in trouble trying to fill in the S and R tables. You may be able to avoid a critical race by re–labeling the states. Try using a grey code to label states. If re–labeling (esp. after merging f–g–h) doesn't work, you may have to add a fourth flip flop.

Here's a general block diagram to consider, for the case of SR latches.

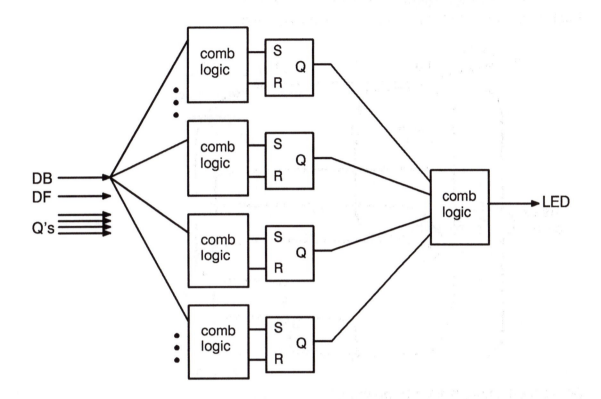

[Can you design the asynchronous sheep lab with enabled toggle flip flops?]

To use the informal **key‒in‒lock** approach of the Supplemental Chapter, or chapter 7 of *DDZO*, start by figuring out what SETs need to occur on the pathway which leads to OUT = 1; you might need **5** SR latches on the SET path. After you have the "key" pathway designed through the set inputs, figure out what condition should RESET each flip flop in the path.

We will test your design by flipping switches that represent DB and DF, and watching the output go HI when the correct input sequence is detected. Once the output goes HI, we will be interested to see if you made sure that the output stays off after we toggle DF back and forth a few times (the **e** to **f** to **a** reset path).

Lab 12

12   Tape Controller

Requirements:

You will simulate a controller for a tape player-recorder.
First build a 2-digit decade counter, which runs from 00 to 99 on
your 2-digit display. The count will represent tape position.
You will have buttons (and lights) for

PLAY	(green)
PAUSE	(yellow)
FAST FORWARD	no lights on
REVERSE	"
RECORD	(red)

In PLAY mode a green light comes on and the counter will advance
at a slow rate until it reaches 99, then it will auto-reverse and
start counting down. When the count reaches 00 during play it
will reverse again and start counting up. In FF mode (no lights
on) the counting will be 4 times faster and always up and when it
reaches 99 it will stop; in REV mode the counting will be fast
down and will stop at 00. No lights are on during FF or REV. Say
FF or REV will override PLAY if either FF or REV are on at the
same time as PLAY. If, during PLAY, the PAUSE button is pushed,
then a yellow light comes on and the counter will stop. There is
a red RECORD light which responds to the REC button but can come
on only during play.

You can build the tape controller in hardware, with the help of a 22V10 PAL, or with Logic-Works or Beige Bag software. In LogicWorks, look at the 74192 BCD up/down counter, a chip with two clock inputs, one for up, one for down. Beige Bag has easier—to—use counters, like the 74169, in its Library, but there may not be a BCD counter. In software the colored LEDs will be replaced with labeled indicators.
If you do Lab 12 with the 22V10, there will be no FTQ!

Digital Design Lab Manual

Lab 13

13　Soo Lock Controller

The Soo Locks, in Sault Ste. Marie, Michigan, bypass the St. Mary's rapids and provide a controlled descent for boats making the 21 foot change in elevation from Lake Superior to Lake Huron. More tonage of shipping pass through the Soo Locks than the Panama Canal or the Suez Canal. To go from Superior to Huron a boat (which can be up to 1000 feet in length) approaches the Superior **gate**. The controller opens a **valve** and water begins filling the lock until the water level is even with the water in Lake Superior. At that time the Superior gate opens and the boat moves into the lock, then the Superior gate closes, and the Superior valve closes. Next the controller opens a valve between the lock and Lake Huron. Water flows out of the lock until the level in the lock is even with Lake Huron. Then the Huron gate opens and the boat moves into Lake Huron. The reverse process occurs if a boat needs to move up from Huron to Superior.

Requirements:

Use LogicWorks or Beige Bag to design a controller for a Soo Lock. Inputs to the controller will be boat detectors on the Superior and Huron side, a water level indicator in the lock, and a boat position indicator. The water level indicator will be an 8-bit counter, as will the boat position indicator. The level of Lake Huron is set to be 30 hex and the level of Lake Superior is set to be C0 hex. The boat position indicator reads 00 when a boat gets to the Superior boat detector, and reads FF when the boat gets to the Huron boat detector. When the boat is safely inside the lock, the boat position indicator reads 7F hex.

The controller has command of a Superior valve and the position of the valve (open or closed) should be shown on the simulation; similarly for command of the Huron valve. Also the controller has command of the Superior gate: when the gate is open the the boat can move between Superior and the lock; similarly for the Huron gate. You would never want to have both gates open simultaneously, nor would it make much sense to have both valves open simultaneously.

In the WAIT state both gates are closed and one valve is open. Depending on whether the boat detector switch goes active for a Superior or Huron boat, either a gate opens right away, or the level in the lock is changed. Both gates close when the boat is safely inside the lock. then the other valve is opened and the water level counter goes either up or down, depending on the valve opened. The gate opens when the lock water is level with one of the two lakes.

If a second boat comes along from the opposite direction while the first boat is being processed, the sequence for the first boat will be completed and the open gate at the end of the sequence will stay open until the second boat gets in the lock.

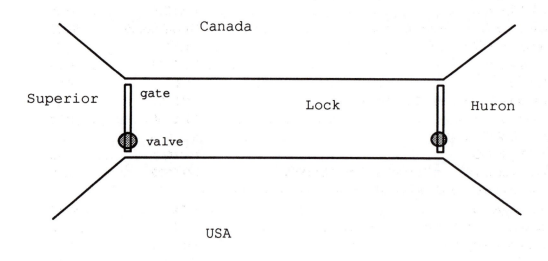

Question: Why not just let water run through big channels from Superior to Huron? Why have this elaborate lock system?

Bag−'o−Chips Kit Inventory

You can use only <u>one</u> of each chip in any design

1. Basic Kit

──────────COMBINATIONAL──────────────────

NAND gates, 4 input gates per chip	7400	$0.45
EXOR gates, 4 per chip	7486	0.55
NOR gates, 4 per chip	7402	0.45
Digital Comparator, 4−bit	7485	0.75
Inverters, 6, Schmitt trigger	7414	0.60
" Open Collector	7406	0.60
" CMOS	74C04	0.40
" 8, TRI−state	74LS240	0.85
Decoder−driver for 7−segment display	7448/DS8856	$2.20
2→1 Multiplexers (4 per chip)	74157	0.65
", inverting	74LS158	0.65
8→1 Multiplexer	74151	0.65
de−Multiplexers, 4 outputs, (2 per chip)	74LS139	0.55
Priority encoder *new for 1990	74LS148	0.74
AND−OR−INVERT, CMOS, Motorola	MC14506	1.35
Majority 3/5, CMOS "	MC14530	1.45
Arithmetic−Logic unit, 4−bit combinatorial, 8 functions	74LS382	2.15

──────────────SEQUENTIAL──────────────────

D−flip flops, two	7474	$0.50
J−K flip flops, old−fashioned, two per chip	7476	0.50
J−K flip flops, 2, negative edge−triggered	74LS112	0.45
latches	74LS174	0.55
Shift register, 8−bit output, serial	74164	0.70
Universal Shift Register	74194	
Shift register, serial−parallel, 4 bit, (2)	74195	0.75
1−shots, (2 per chip)	74LS123	0.60
Binary counter, 4−bit, up/down	74169	1.40
Memory, 1024 x 4 static RAM, TRI−state outputs	21C14	0.70
or inmos CMOS chip, 4K x 4, 45 nsec access time (1991)	1423P	2.78

or new SRAM for 1997... ────────────────────────────

Timer	555	0.55
Operational Amplifier, (2 per chip) **REQUIRES ±12 VOLTS**	LF353	1.05
NPN transistor	2N4401	0.45
V−MOS FET transistor, Siliconix, n−channel enhancement mode	VN40A D/F	0.95
5 x 4 matrix keyboard	TI 11 KS 121	$2.80
7−seg display, 3 digit, common cathode, multiplexed	HP 5082−7433	**$8.48 ouch!**
Lignt−emitting diodes (LED's), 3, different colors		0.20 ea
8−position DIP switches, <u>2 per kit</u>		1.20 ea
toggle switches, miniature, two		1.50
potentiometer, 10−20KΩ		2.05

Digital Design Lab Manual

Wire strippers . . . . Miller # 100 . . . . 2.75

solderless breadboards, <u>three</u>, **individually numbered** . . . . Global, EXP . . . . $7.95 ea

NOTEs: (1) **Diodes (1N914** & **Schottky)** & **resistors** (100Ω, 1K, 10K, 20K, 100K, 1MΩ) will be available from drawers in the lab; **capacitors** are available from large spools near the coat rack.

(2) Use the **Weller** soldering iron in the lab to connect wires to the keyboard, toggle switch and potentiometer; remember to keep the soldering sponge wet!

2nd set of parts

Pick Up These Chips After You Finish Lab 5

Transparent latches, 3−state, 8 bit, non−inverting . . . . 74LS**373** 2.00

Binary counter, 4−bit, up/down, 3−state, async clear, AMD . . . . 25LS2**569** 3.00

EPROM 8K x 8−bit output, pre−programmed for labs 6C, C, D, E . . . . . 27 64 or − 512 . . . . . . 7.00

    (Either a 2764 or **27512** EPROM...note '512 address pins)

Registered PAL . . . . **22V10 (CE)** 8.00

True HEX display, with built in decoder−driver & latch (1992) . . . . HP **7340** $24.97

Comparator, analog−to−digital . . . . LM311 . . . . 0.65

R−2R ladder & analog switches, + latch for 8−bit multiplying DAC . . . . AD**7524** 4.00

Voltage−Controlled Oscillator . . . . AD**654** 6.60

dynamic RAM, 256K x 4, 100 nsec access time, Motorola (new in '91) . . MCM**514256** 5.85

solderless breadboards, <u>**two more**</u>, **individually numbered** . . . . Global . . . . $7.95 ea

AFTER LAB B:

8−bit A/D converter . . . . AD**7576** $7.10

ALU, 4−bit . . . . 74**181** 2.05

piezoelectric crystal (no data sheet) . . . . DIGIKEY 3.50

<u>. . . . . YOU MAY RECEIVE THE ROM & HEX DISPLAY ON A 600−SERIES BREADBOARD</u>

Each student will receive a power supply ($42), logic probe ($18) and Wavetek digital multimeter DM27XT ($119, "Have you hugged your multimeter today?"). The logic probe and power supply will be available when you pick out your "basic inventory" chips after Lab Zero; **The multimeter can be checked out after you complete lab 4 and are ready to start lab 5.**

Note about logic probes: Refrain from flexing the power wires on the logic probe at the place where they enter the probe body. After too much flexing one of the wires will "open circuit" and the power connection will have to be re−soldered.

Rolls of colored wire (22 gauge solid core hook−up, Belden), costing about $8.00 per 100−ft., will be available on spools. And 24 gauge wire in 25−conductor sections, donated by the Telecommunications Dept. at Brown Univ, is available too.

Data Sheets

20 pages of general information, then data sheets follow in the order of the basic inventory list. Parts from the extended inventory are described later in the data sheets. Ignore page numbers on data sheets.

The last item is Am 2909 Sequencer data sheets.
The data sheets, <u>but not the chip</u>, are needed for lab D.
You will receive "Feeling Comfortable With Logic Analyzers" (FCWLA, written by HP) after lab 5. **Please return FCWLA when you finish the course.**

It is not necessary to understand *everything* in the data sheets; the pinout is the most important information. Transfer pinouts to 3 x 5 cards for convenience. See Supplemental chapters 1 and 2 for more explanation of chip parameters.

Most of the TTL data sheets are from the **Signetics** catalog. Other US manufacturers which have provided data sheets are **Analog Devices, National Semiconductor, Texas Instruments, Motorola, Intel, Siliconix & AMD = Advanced Micro Devices.** Some memory data sheets are from SGS Thomson (inmos).

If any of the data sheets are illegible, see JD. The copy process can filter out high frequency fine print.

~~178 pages 6/7/89~~
~~190 pages 6/6/90~~
~~218 pages 6/6/91~~
223 pages 5/20/92
200 pages 1995
215 pages in 1996

INDEX

Numbers

A

B

C

D

E

F

G

H

Notes

Notes

Notes

Notes

Notes

Notes

Notes

Notes

Notes